DEEPER

STILL

Ministry Empowered by the Holy Spirit

Dr. CJ Rhodes

Publihhed by :
Relentless Publishing House, LLC
www.relentlesspublishing.com

ISBN: 9781948829434

First Edition: March 2020

10 9 8 7 6 5 4 3 2 1

Dedication

To the born again sons and daughters of Africa at the
vanguard of another Great Awakening.

Table of Contents

PREFACE

This book is a culmination of years of discernment. I grew up as Missionary Baptist in a Mississippi railroad town. After a season of adolescent agnosticism, I was radically called to salvation and later to ministry among Pentecostals whose openness to the surprising work of the Holy Spirit "sooth[ed] my doubts and calm[ed] my fears," as the Andre Crouch song "The Blood Will Never Lose Its Power" testifies. After experiencing the power of God among them, I later returned to my native Black Baptist roots, now ablaze with Holy Ghost power in a way I previously deemed unavailable in the religion of my youth. This formation in both Baptist and Pentecostal settings made me feel odd and I was often called to choose a side by well-meaning saints in each denominational tribe. What follows in these pages is the way I reconciled these two ways of being Christian by placing Calvary and Pentecost in dialog.

This is also a testament to that journey and a reminder that I was never alone in it. During my time at Duke Divinity School, for example, I was introduced to Charles Price Jones by my favorite professor, Dr. William C. Turner. Turner grew up in the United Holy Church of America and has pastored Mt. Level Missionary Baptist Church since 1990. It was he who taught me how to negotiate my Christian identity relative to Baptist distinctives with a more charismatic pneumatology. By God's providence, I would later be called to serve Mt. Helm Baptist Church, where Jones served during the birthing of the Holiness revival he, Charles Harrison Mason, and others led in Jackson, MS. Because of my studies at Duke, I consumed everything I could about this man who shaped my life from an historical distance.

My fondness for Jones the reformer and renewalist was articulated in the dissertation I composed in partial completion of my Doctor of Ministry degree awarded from Wesley Biblical Seminary. This book is a greatly revised version of that composition. It examines the Holy Spirit-empowered reform ministry of Charles Price Jones and commends it to contemporary Black Baptist pastors and preachers.

My hope is that Bapticostals— Baptists unapologetic about the synthesis of Word and Spirit— serving in traditional settings will especially be liberated to offer transformative leadership for the Church and society as a result of the encouragement found in these pages. To be sure, this work is not a clarion call to remove these churches from their denominational homes in order to join other movements. I desire to see revival and renewal in Black Baptist churches, associations, and conventions. I want for Spirit-empowered Baptist churches to catch on fire with the zeal of the Lord so that evangelism, social action, passionate worship, and deep repentance will not only respond to the crisis of dying churches, but also will better serve fragmented communities and hopeless people yearning for a word from the Lord. As that great hymn of the church pleads,

Revive us again;

Fill each heart with Thy love;
May each soul be rekindled
With fire from above.

Hallelujah! Thine the glory.
Hallelujah! Amen.
Hallelujah! Thine the glory.
Revive us again.

INTRODUCTION

Deeper, deeper, blessed Holy Spirit,
Take me deeper still,
Till my life is wholly lost in Jesus,
And His perfect will.

Charles Price Jones, "Deeper, Deeper"

"Help me, Holy Ghost!" and "I feel my help!" punctuate the celebratory closes of Black Baptist sermons any given Sunday. Unfortunately, in some Baptist circles the Holy Spirit receives less attention throughout the preparation and most of the delivery of messages that are nevertheless biblically sound and Christ-exalting. This is not to say that the average Black Baptist pastor does not believe in the Holy Spirit. Like other Trinitarians, Baptists affirm the Lord and Giver of life, as revealed in Scripture, and attested to in church covenants and confessions. But because many traditional Baptists have historically been by practice and emphasis "Jesus people," acknowledgement of the "shy member" of the Trinity is rare, sermon closes notwithstanding.

Certainly, this isn't true of all Black Baptists. There are many preachers and pastors within our tradition who have a robust doctrine of the Holy Spirit and who live that out in their personal lives and ministries. At the risk of caricaturing my tribe, though, I must admit that in too many cases I've seen "Spirit-talk" ridiculed, mocked, or played with. I've been in too many settings where fellow Baptists disparage any talk about the work of the Holy Spirit outside of convicting and regenerating sinners. Being led by, filled with, and under the influence of the Comforter seems too "Pentecostal" for those who see members of the Sanctified church as ignorant holy rollers driven more by emotionalism than by sound biblical exposition. Such conjectures have long forced a wedge between Baptists, with some Spirit-focused ones even leaving their home churches and denominations in order to feel more welcomed and freer elsewhere.

But the culture is shifting. Growing numbers of Gen X and Millennial preachers and pastors within the various National Baptist Conventions are unapologetically expressing a deepening appreciation for the Holy Spirit's power and presence in Gospel ministry. They are less reticent to publicly express their Baptist convictions while simultaneously describing some experiences more associated with Pentecostals and Charismatics, sensing no contradiction between Baptist distinctives and tongues, divine healing, and prophetic words. Hence, the term Bapticostal is sometimes playfully or seriously used to distinguish these Baptists from cessationist brothers and sisters who deny the ongoing presence of all the spiritual gifts Paul lists in 1 Corinthians 12-14. Said differently, Bapticostals are Baptists who hold to historic Baptist doctrines and polity and stand along a spectrum of beliefs affirming the present need for the gifts, fruit, and manifest presence of the Holy Spirit.

Due to the rates of retirements among Baby Boomer pastors, many of these younger leaders are being called to serve declining churches in need of revitalization. They are not called to the churches because they are Bapticostal, mind you, but because their talents are readily visible to the members of the search committees who select them. Sadly, due to the enormous stresses of these plateaued or dying ministry contexts, many of these young pastors reach burnout by the third year and, feeling defeated, leave the church for other ministry opportunities, if they remain in ministry at all.[1] One observation is that all too often the pragmatic skills that made the preacher marketable to the congregation are insufficient for the Goliath-sized problems they endure almost immediately. Seminary trained pastors soon discover their degrees did not suitably prepare them; preachers schooled in the hard knocks also find themselves frustrated by the overwhelming burden of leading stiff-necked people. Born of necessity and biblical study, many of these Gospel messengers are more open toward so-called charismatic experiences because through them they encounter a realm of spiritual breakthrough and power of which they were previously unaware.

Much of this enthusiasm for a more charismatic Baptist faith is due to the persuasive success of the Full Gospel Baptist Church Fellowship International, which was birthed out of the National Baptist Convention USA in the 1990's. This movement's mission was to "give Baptists the

---

[1] According to a LifeWay Research survey of 1,500 evangelical and historically black church pastors, "Though pastors are stressed about money and overwhelming ministry demands, only one percent abandon the pulpit each year." Nevertheless, that same survey offers that though pastoral abandonment is rare, pastoral turnover is not: "Most said they moved on because they had taken the previous church as far as they could (54 percent). However, 23 percent of pastors who changed churches say they left because of conflict in the church." For more information on this study, see "Despite Stresses, Few Pastors Give Up on Ministry" (LifeWay Research, https://lifewayresearch.com/2015/09/01/despite-stresses-few-pastors-give-up-on-ministry/. September 1, 2005.) The survey itself is titled "Pastor Protection Research Study: Survey of 1,500 Pastors (http://lifewayresearch.com/wp-content/uploads/2015/08/Pastor-Protection-Quantitative-Report-Final.pdf).

right to choose" and masses of leaders and members were liberated to what they considered to be a fuller experience of the divine. As will be explored in greater detail later in this book, younger Baptist preachers coming of age over the last two decades embrace expressions and theological positions that a century ago were condemned as "unsound" Baptist doctrine, and much of this can be credited to this movement, even if a number of us have not joined it. Moreover, an unbiased study of Baptist history will show that Baptists and Pentecostals are second cousins estranged by denominational battles, for much of what goes for Afro-Pentecostalism is traceable to pre-Reconstruction era Black Baptist experience. What is needed, then, is an affirmation of this reality so that more Afro-Baptists can be renewed in their ministries by the fullness of the Holy Spirit without feeling compelled to join other reformations. Pastors in traditional Baptist settings need no longer apologize for desiring or having a "Pentecostal experience." This book is an attempt to get us delivered!

Providentially, my present fondness for the reforms Charles Price Jones made is related in part to my spiritual and ministerial genealogy. After receiving my call to ministry, I announced it to Bishop Arnold Stanton, pastor and founder of New Life Cathedral of Worship in Hazlehurst, MS. Stanton was a rising star in the Church of Christ (Holiness) USA, the denomination Jones founded, before launching out to establish an independent church. After founding New Life as an essentially independent Holiness church, Stanton entertained a more neo-Pentecostal approach to the ministry that would come to define the church's doctrine and worship culture by the time I arrived. Growing up within a Missionary Baptist context with a brief connection in a United Methodist church, and later being formed by New Life, my life is in many interesting ways emblematic of the kind of Spirit-empowered ministry most readily seen in the life of Charles Price Jones, a Baptist reformer who took Holy Ghost help seriously. In college I returned to my Baptist roots by serving two Missionary Baptists congregations. At Clear Creek Missionary Baptist Church, I was known for powerful praying and a spiritual walk that magnetized many members. I recall an occasion wherein I prayed during an altar call and a word of knowledge came to me about a member planning to commit suicide after service. I obeyed God and called it out, praying for the emotional healing and hope needed to rescue that child of God from death. It was later confirmed to me that such a person was there, had planned to commit suicide after service, but God blocked it! The other church was led by the late Julius Minor and Ethel Young-Minor (now Scurlock) who were friendly to the Full Gospel Baptist movement and who celebrated both my intellect and spiritual giftedness. They were the first Baptist ministers who affirmed the Bapitcostal identity taking shape in my life and ministry. I now celebrate this spiritual understanding in ways I was nervous to do more than a decade ago.

The Purpose

This book is my testimony and a charge. Through a brief tour of history and engagement with current trends in the Body of Christ, I offer a glimpse into one Bapticostal's self-awareness and hope for the renewal of the Black Baptist tradition. For most of my time in ministry I have felt a sense of exile, of not fully fitting into the rigid boxes denominationalists categorize us by. I'm too Baptist for some Pentecostals and to Charismatic for some Baptists. The way forward is something integral to the meaning, message, and model of Spirit-driven baptized believers who know something is lacking in our present configurations and are anointed to reform, revitalize, and renew churches and communities as a result.

In order to illustrate this mission for the present age, this work retrieves and critically assumes lessons from one of our own who knew it would take academic learning and Holy Ghost burning to lead God's people from spiritual, moral, and political ruin. The succeeding chapters will provide meaningful rationales for affirming Jones as an exemplary model for study. The book will advance in three movements. First, I share biblical, theological, and historical research that addresses the classical understanding of the Baptist church and its leaders; the genealogy of pastoral vocation in Black Baptist churches; and missional theology and postmodern apologetics. Second, I offer a theological and sociopolitical historic survey of pastoral leadership that will contextualize the state of the Black Church in Mississippi during the time of Charles Price Jones. Third, more contemporary discussions and debates about Jones' legacy within Black Baptist circles will be engaged, which will briefly look at Martin Luther King Jr. and the Civil Rights Movements as well as Paul Morton and the Full Gospel Baptist Church Fellowship reformation. Finally, based upon the previous material I venture toward a Bapticostal identity that is relevant to present and future needs for spiritual revitalization, social transformation, and ecclesial reformation.

The scope of the research for the dissertation upon which this book is based was limited to Jones' tenure at Mt. Helm and the broader conversation about Black pastoral leadership he was engaged in at the time and beyond. I will not seek to resolve other important historical, theological, and institutional questions that I anticipate emerging in response to the matters raised here. Ultimately, I affirm a non-cessationist, thus continuationist and charismatic pneumatology and place it in creative tension within the Black Baptist tradition. It is my hope that this book will provide much needed context for contemporary pastoral crises among and within Black communities; provide some constructive appraisals of present pastoral models while offering adaptive ones based on a Spirit-empowered model; and assist younger pastors in revitalizing dying churches and/or promote the planting of new congregations that are missionally driven for the sake of personal salvation and social transformation.

May the Holy Spirit renew the Church.

1

Black Baptists and Spiritual Leadership

Introduction

With the passing of Clay Evans in 2019, I was reminded
of how his kind of Baptist identity was in stark contrast to
that of Joseph H. Jackson, the former towering President of
the National Baptist Convention USA, Inc. Both natives of
the South, their tenures in Chicago were marked by
completely divergent styles in worship, preaching, and
social engagement. Jackson was more reserved, mimicking
the "high church" culture of many affluent white mainline
congregations. Evans, on the other hand, retained passionate
Black folk religion and even embraced elements of
Pentecostalism, as attested by a church historian who claims
"Clay Evans moved into some of that [neo-Pentecostal
worship style]." He continues, "Clay Evans [saw] over a
thousand people on Sunday morning but Olivet,
Monumental, and Pilgrim, who used to see thousands of
people, if they can see a couple of hundred [were] happy."[2]
The divergence in style and substance between these two
notable National Baptist pastors did not spring forth *ex*

---

[2] Aldon D. Morris and Shayne Lee, *Church, Identity, and Change*, 370.

nihilo. They are but two examples of the lingering dialog and debate between different African American Baptist sensibilities. William Faulkner stated in Requiem for a Nun, "The past isn't dead. It isn't even the past." To understand these ongoing debates among Baptists about spiritual gifts and worship styles, for instance, we must travel back to the 1800's to get a glimpse of where such debates began. Any serious student of Black church history will soon discover that the 1890's and early 1900's were critical for how Black Baptists drew the line in the sand around certain pneumatological understandings in order to distance themselves from or renew notions of Christian spirituality they inherited from slavery.

"It's Got to Mean More than a Shout": Reforming the Black Baptist Pastorate after Reconstruction

That people of African descent in America are Christians is both mesmerizing and miraculous. The horrors of chattel slavery, the unborn hope of Reconstruction, the legalized racial terrorism of Jim Crow and its lingering sociopolitical affects are enough to turn Blacks away from a religion that played an inordinate part in every epoch of our social misery. Yet, what the enemy meant for evil, God made good. From the crucible of America's racial imagination came the so-called "Black church" and its necessary, though complicated leaders, Black pastors. Their role in the spiritual, moral, political, and economic strivings of the race was punctuated in the 1890's when Confederate sympathizers consolidated political power and wholly disenfranchised Blacks of their civil and political rights earned after the Civil War and bolstered constitutionally through the era of Reconstruction. With the future of the Black community in jeopardy, Black pastors were called upon to be the voice of a people in search of hope. Black

Baptists were illustrative in the quest for pastoral power, in more ways than one.

Black Baptist Reformations in Mississippi

In places like Mississippi, Baptists reign supreme. You can hear many African Americans throughout the state boast, "I'm Baptist born, Baptist bred, and when I die, I'll be Baptist dead." In *Religion in Mississippi* Randy J. Sparks speaks about connections between American revivalism, Africanism, and the creative forging of postbellum Black religious life as variables contributing to their exponential growth.[3] Juan Williams and Quinton Dixie note, "At the close of the Civil War, Black Baptist membership was an estimated 250,000. By 1890 the number had increased to roughly 1,350,000." "Despite this tremendous growth," they continue, "Black Baptists were widely criticized by blacks and whites from other denominations."[4] Due in part to their being seen by the larger culture as uneducated and primitive, some Baptist pastors began to cast a modern vision of advancement that provoked a civil war between the old and the new. Two dominant but competing sides emerged, generally called the "progressives" and the "conservatives."

---

[3] Sparks continues: "Religious practices formerly hidden in the "invisible church" became a vital part of postbellum institutional worship. Though some of these practices originated in the Great Revival, others clearly reflected African religious traditions. Among the beliefs and practices with African roots were visionary conversion experiences, or "travelin'." Another Africanism was the ring shout, still broadly practiced during the Reconstruction era, which by that time was called, at least by one scholar, "the Heavenly dance." To be sure, these practices were similar to non-black Primitive Baptist churches and not limited to black Baptists, though there were clear stylistic and theological divergences here and there. (144-145)

[4] *This Far by Faith: Stories from the African American Religious Experience* (William Marrow, 2003), 136.

The progressives were clergy who believed that liberal arts education and respectability politics would help advance the race both religiously and socially.[5] They were ashamed of "slave religion" as they became educated, refined assimilationists. Conservatives, on the other hand, wanted to preserve "old time religion" and were willing to forfeit or minimize upward social mobility in order to retain a more fundamentalist understanding of the New Testament church and religious sensibilities associated with slavery. Their resistance to change caused them to be viewed as impediments to Black success. Today, we can see the two "kinds" of Baptists who are heirs to this division. Baptist clergy who pride themselves on accredited seminary training, social respectability, political activism, and dignified worship continue the progressive legacy, while clergy who eschew seminary (calling it the "cemetery"), worldly affairs like politics, and who celebrate enthusiastic preaching are heirs of the conservatives. As it was in the 1890's, the latter group still outnumbers the former. And yet there were then and now "other" Baptists who do not neatly fit the progressive/conservative binary. Respecting elements of both camps, these Baptist pastors offer us a more excellent way. One such preacher was Charles Price Jones.

Charles Price Jones as Baptist Reformer and Renewalist

Charles Price Jones (December 9, 1865 – January 19, 1949), became the fifth pastor of Mt. Helm Baptist Church in 1895. His tenure there was a crucible for a moderating view between progressive learning and conservative

---

[5] See Evelyn Brooks Higginbotham's *Righteous Discontent: The Women's Movement in the Black Baptist Church, 1880-1920* for more on respectability politics and the black church.

burning. Jones has been neglected in historical and theological studies, eclipsed by his co-laborer Charles Harrison Mason and other reformers of that era. He is still celebrated in the Church of Christ (Holiness) USA, the denomination he founded, but is relatively unknown elsewhere. Thankfully, various historians in recent times have written about Jones and provide stunning evidence that he was seeking to take Baptists to their theological extremes but not beyond what could be found in the New Testament.[6]

It may have been unexpected that Jones would be a reformer emphasizing a deeper spiritual life in God that would issue forth in holiness and Holy Ghost power. In *Bishop C. H. Mason and the Roots of the Church of God in Christ*, Ithiel C. Clemmons notes, "Jones emerged a cosmopolitan, creative, self-contained leader of unbendable conviction."[7] As a refined, well-educated Baptist pastor who sought to revitalize the spiritual integrity and zeal of the church and convention, "Jones never intended to leave the Baptist pastorate."[8] But his dissatisfaction with nominal faith and encroaching denominationalism drew him into a spiritual revolution that would associate him with the Holiness movement and ultimately force him out of his native tradition. Indeed, Jones and his co-laborers

---

[6] Recent scholarship also demonstrates that the Holiness preacher received much support from other Baptist pastors and the majority of members of Mount Helm Baptist Church. *Charles Price Jones: First Black Holiness Reformer,* edited by Anita Bingham Jefferson, provides several of Jones' own works and words. *Moving Forward on God's Highway* by Willenham Castilla, and Ithiel Clemmons' *Bishop C. H. Mason and the Roots of the Church of God in Christ* are reliable presentations of Jones' reforms from both a Holiness and a Pentecostal perspective.

[7] Clemmons, 17.

[8] Ibid.

"understood the radical, prophetic vision of the mainline black churches was essential to break through the ironclad systems of cruelty that oppressed a whole race of people. But attempting to fight the goliath of racism and white supremacy without spiritual sustenance was, they said, to enter the battle without adequate resources."[9] Retrieving the best of the conservatives' reliance on the Spirit and marrying that with the progressives' reasoned and radical religion led to the birth of a revival that still kindles heads and hearts today.

"It Rises and Falls on Leadership": Spiritual Sources of Leadership Formation in Contemporary Black Baptist Pastoral Identities

Contemporary pastors seeking answers to complex leadership questions often turn to secular sources or chase the latest conference. While popular books and conferences can be helpful and fruitful, sometimes they do not touch on the spiritual empowerment critical for effectuating lasting change and surviving the warfare it entails. The indwelling power and presence of the Holy Spirit in the life and leadership of Black Baptist pastors is neglected in large measure because within the last few decades we have settled for pragmatic strategies, seduced into thinking that if we just apply the right program, we will have instant success.

Another pressing issue is some Baptists are uneasy talking about the Holy Spirit outside of salvation and regeneration following the emergence and explosive growth of the Pentecostal/Charismatic/Neo-Pentecostal movements. I aver that it is past time for a more serious look at the Holy

---

[9] Ibid., 21.

Spirit from a non-cessationist position, however. The shifting views in the Southern Baptist Convention (SBC), with half of their pastors saying tongues are valid today,[10] and the increased academic interests in Baptist charismatic or continualist pneumatology should signal to my tribe that we can no longer afford to be dismissive or nonchalant about this matter. Furthermore, the emergence and sustained popularity of the Full Gospel Baptist Church Fellowship International has created a space for dialog about the state of these divisions. Though popular and widely read Bible teacher John MacArthur is avidly against charismatic pneumatology as his books *Charismatic Chaos* and *Strange Fire* explicate, many other Reformed and Baptist authors both affirm and celebrate the gifts of the Spirit. Craig Keener,[11] Sam Storms,[12] Wayne Grudem,[13] D. A. Carson,[14] and Gregg Allison[15] all provide solid exegetical and theological warrant for an evangelical doctrine of all spiritual gifts, providing greater to lesser degrees of comfort with the larger charismatic movement. In *Discipleship for African American Christians: A Journey through the Church Covenant*, William C. Turner elucidates the role of the Spirit in the life of Baptist Christians and churches while also being

---

[10] SBC poll: Half of pastors say 'tongues' valid. Christian Century. 6/26/2007, Vol. 124 Issue 13, p 13-13. 3/4p.

[11] *Spirit Hermeneutics: Reading Scripture in Light of Pentecost* (Grand Rapids, MI: Eerdmans, 2016); *Gift and Giver: The Holy Spirit for Today.*

[12] *Practicing the Power: Welcoming the Gifts of the Holy Spirit in Your Life; The Beginners Guide to Spiritual Gifts.*

[13] *Systematic Theology.*

[14] *Showing the Spirit: A Theological Exposition of 1 Corinthians 12-14.*

[15] *Sojounrers and Strangers: The Doctrine of the Church.*

both critical and irenic toward Pentecostal pneumatology. Furthermore, Vinson Synan's *The Century of the Holy Spirit: 100 Years of Pentecostal and Charismatic Renewal* highlights the history of Baptist renewal with an emphasis on charismatic activity within Baptist origins.[16] He notes, "Baptist historian Edward Hiscox points to early records of the Philadelphia association where there are indications that various gifts of the Spirit were in operation in the churches of that area about 1743."[17] Though Black Baptists largely became cessationists after Reconstruction, Baptist reformers like Charles Price Jones sought to restore the Church of Christ through pastoral leadership infused with the Spirit's fullness. Only a Spirit-anointed pastorate will make a qualitative difference in the kind of ecclesial and social leadership our communities desperately need in this postmodernizing era. Ours is a time to reclaim and prioritize it for the good of the church and to the glory of God.

Conclusion

Barbara Dianne Savage affirms, "During Reconstruction, Black communities established their own churches, primarily Baptist, throughout the South. Many of those who emerged as Black political leaders were ministers, empowered by their literacy and by their prominent role in building the Black churches which served as the first forums for collective political organizing."[18] Today's Black church wrestles with the continued relevance of pastoral leadership in and out of the pulpit. As the centuries-long debate about

---

[16] Synan, 84-192.

[17] Ibid., 185.

[18] Your Sprit Walks Beside Us,4.

pastoral training and authority continues, serious consideration of the indwelling presence and gifts of the Holy Spirit provides an important corrective to leadership formation models that are heavy on leadership theory but meager on spiritual distinctiveness. A "learning and burning" model of pastoral and preaching ministry is suitable for the crisis the Black church now faces. With these things in mind, we move forward by looking afresh at one such "learning and burning" exemplar and the lessons his ministry has for us today and in the future.

I want for Spirit-empowered Baptist churches to catch on fire with the zeal of the Lord.

2

LEARNING AND BURNING: CHARLES PRICE JONES AS A BLACK BAPTIST REFORMER

Introduction

There is an enduring debate about whether leaders are born or made. In the case of Charles Price Jones, maybe both claims are true. Jones was born for such a time as the one he occupied, and he served his generation and Lord in Spirit and truth. The lingering realties of chattel slavery and the ensuing evils of Jim Crow segregation provided the stage upon which Jones served. But life experiences, understanding of Scripture and desire for more of God's manifest power shaped him in ways that called him from the status quo. This chapter situates Jones within the sociopolitical history wherein the future of Black Baptist identity was contested, offering my perspective on how the reformer met the ecclesial and social challenges of his time with an emphasis on pneumatology. I submit that we can glean from this the origins of Bapticostal renewal.

"In the Days When Hope Unborn Had Died": Black Subjugation After Reconstruction, 1875-1890

The Reconstruction era was short lived in Mississippi. Intriguingly, Blacks had little to no education or economic resources after Emancipation but during Reconstruction the collective genius of Black Mississippians intimidated those who feared the destabilization of White power. By 1875, only ten years after the War, White supremacists terrorized the Magnolia State in order to "redeem" it from the Negro and the "nigger lovers" who collaborated with them for racial progress. W.S. Scarborough, in the *Christian Recorder*, makes this point clear:

> The trouble is the Negro is advancing too rapidly for many of the white-liners of the South, and there is a determination to call a halt. Consequently, all sorts of schemes are devised to impede the progress of the blacks. They are shot down if they testify against white men they meet the same fate if they refuse to do so. If they attempt to assert their civil and political rights in any manly way they are mobbed, butchered, and killed. If they nominate or assist in nominating one of their own number to office, it matters not how well qualified he may be, a cry is raised that "Negroes are drawing the race issue." The Negro has been patient—yes, more than this; he has prostrated himself at the feet of the government, and has remonstrated with it to give him protection in the enjoyment of his rights. The Government has utterly failed to do its duty, in that it has disregarded his

request.[19]

Scarborough penned this in 1891, a year after Mississippi passed into law the new state constitution, which replaced the more progressive Constitution of 1868. Though the new constitution's introductory sentence promised that it would be an exercise in democratic empowerment for all citizens, Black and White alike, a nefarious doctrine hid within its pages. Article 12, which addresses the right to vote, implies the racist motivations of the drafters. But if the language of the 1890 Constitution is not convincing enough, the actual sentiments of those present at the Constitutional Convention, or who commented positively on it, should leave no doubt that it intended to seal de jure segregation and Black subjugation. In an altogether powerful text, Neil R. McMillen's *Dark Journey: Black Mississippians in the Age of Jim Crow* evidences the racist antecedents:

> Rarely circumspect, James K. Vardaman saw no reason to deny the framers' [of the 1890 Constitution] intent: "There is no use to equivocate or lie about the matter…. Mississippi's constitutional convention of 1890 was held for no other purpose than to eliminate the nigger from politics' not the 'ignorant and vicious,' as some of those apologists would have you believe, but the nigger… Let the world know it just as it is." The point was also underscored in the white press. Black education progress notwithstanding, the *Clarion-Ledger* predicted, whites would never again permit Black

---

[19] *A Documentary History of the Negro People in the United States, Volume 2: From Reconstruction to the Founding of the N.A.A.C.P.*, ed. Herbert Aptheker, Citadel Press (1992), 751-752.

enfranchisement. "They do not object to negros voting on account of ignorance, but on account of color."[20]

Essentially, the 1890 Constitution legalized schemes to deter and deny political and economic rights provided to Black citizens of Mississippi from 1868 to that point. This disenfranchisement and consequential disempowerment were based solely upon the diabolical logic of White domination.

Where Do We Go From Here?: Debating the Future of the Afro-Baptist Pulpit After Reconstruction

The broader sociopolitical realities of that era called upon the unique leadership of the Black church, though debates about how that leadership should progress intensified during the post-Reconstruction period. Barbara Dianne Savage observes, "[t]he opening decades of the twentieth century also were marked by an intellectual clash between education and belief, modernity and religion, science and faith, the intellectual and the spiritual."[21] Baptist leaders contending for the future of the pastorate fell on opposing sides of those clashes. Building on the denominational evolution of Reconstruction era Baptists, the younger cadre of leaders charted an accommodationist-nationalistic dialectic for survival in the 1890's and at the dawning of the twentieth century. They were not alone in these efforts. Elias Camp Morris, the first president of the National Baptist Convention, which was organized in 1895,

---

[20] Ibid., 43.

[21] *Your Spirits Walk Beside Us,* 7.

shouted this message from the regional and national stages afforded him. In his Educational Sermon, preached in 1894 (prior to becoming NBC president) at the Baptist Educational Convention at Montgomery, AL, Morris averred:

> For years the Negro Baptists of the world have been held up to the ridicule of the other denominations. Their ministers have been classed as the most ignorant of the race and their manner of worship has been called a modified form of heathenism. This grave charge has stood before the world for a generation. But I tell you tonight that the charge was never true of us as a whole, for from the days of slavery until now, the leading Baptist preachers and the intelligent and progressive element in our churches have composed the vanguard of God's great army among the Negro Christians of the world.[22]

What Morris terms "heathenism" is also called "slave religion" by contemporary scholars. From the 1870's on there was, as Savage puts it, "profound unease with the legacy of spiritual practices of enslaved people, a cultural heritage that many viewed as antiquated, primitive, tainted by the sins of slavery, and marked by pagan retentions from Africa."[23] That younger Blacks, the second generation after Emancipation, were at the vanguard of the progressive reforms, speaks to the embarrassment they felt toward their enslaved ancestors. As educated and enlightened people

---

[22] Morris, E. C., *Sermons, Addresses and Reminiscences*, 17.

[23] *Their Spirits Walk Beside Us*, 6.

vying for dignity in the Jim Crow South, they insisted on reformations that emulated the middle-class White church. John M. Giggie points out the range of expressions and beliefs the progressives assailed: "ecstatic worship and a popular faith in the supernatural widespread during bondage and still part of many Delta communities. In particular, they desperately wanted members to resist breaking spontaneously into bouts of shrieking, crying, dancing, hand-clapping, and foot stomping during services. Nothing, they asserted, smacked of disorderliness more than impulsive behavior and open exhibits of unchecked emotion."[24]

To enforce these reforms, the progressive led associations and conventions demanded member churches to allow them to vet potential preachers to see if they were fit for ministry. They cultivated something like a Presbyterian model for pastoral licensing, such that the preacher's license came not from a local congregation but from the Association. That the strident requirements for licensure and ordination included prerequisite literacy and education, the appeal for learned clergy was fought vigorously by conservative preachers who believed this usurped local church autonomy. They also challenged, even if uncritically, progressive attempts to get rid of African-styled folk religion. On these grounds conservatives "insisted on the right to appoint their own preachers, regardless of educational level; set their own styles of worship and music; and recognize spiritual authority in a variety of ways, including supernatural communication."[25] To be clear, the

---

[24] *After Redemption*, 179.

[25] Ibid., 180.

conservatives believed in the immediacy of Spirit that they refused to surrender to progressive bureaucracy. They were in the majority because, as Clemmons points out, "The black church from its inception in the United States has been in part grounded in pneumatological experience. They realized the need of the power of the Spirit to confront political structures and social and economic systems[.]"[26]

To many observers, there were only these two options for the Black church, one charted by the conservatives and the other reformed by the progressives. Into this debate between progressive and conservative Black Baptists came a third option, however, one I call "radical reform." Trained as a progressive and holding on to elements of conservative spirituality, Charles Price Jones models this third way.

A New Baptist Vanguard: Charles Price Jones' "More Excellent Way"

Pointing to the "generation gap" between both parties, Carter G. Woodson wrote about "a conservative majority and a progressive minority within the African American churches," who "fought to control the future of Black Christianity."[27] Jones, however, offered a more dialectical approach. Giggie is right when he states that leaders like Jones and others like him "offered a compromise position that appealed to moderate men and women who preferred a combination of ideas from both camps."[28] What held these contributions from both camps together was Jones' emphasis

---

[26] Clemmons, 29.

[27] *Rise to Respectability*, 4.

[28] Giggie, 180.

27

on the Holy Spirit. If the conservatives were dangerous because they were "so heavenly minded that they were no earthly good," Jones was afraid that the progressives were fast approaching a self-help Deism without supernatural power. To be sure, Jones was an advocate for education and entrepreneurship, himself being a highly educated preacher. Nevertheless, his own spiritual crisis led him to the conviction that the people of God needed something beyond education; they needed something within. What is most known today about Jones is that he was an ardent preacher of Holiness and cast his doctrine in the tenor of Wesleyan perfectionism, which in important ways contradicted Baptist's historic doctrine of sanctification. His extremist views on certain points cannot be denied. Elias Camp Morris, one of Jones' mentors and pastors, would in 1899 preach a national presidential address implicitly condemning his former student's doctrinal aberration. But there is more to this story than a Baptist-turned-Holiness preacher. In fact, Jones had every intention of remaining a Baptist the remainder of his life. In *History of Church of Christ (Holiness) U.S.A. 1895-1965*, O.B. Cobbins contends "Bishop C.P. Jones was a staunch Baptist himself, having pastored in Alabama, Arkansas, and in Mississippi[.]"[29] By Jones' own account, he never intended to leave the Baptist church:

> I had never thought of living or dying anything but a Baptist, but I had been taught that a Baptist was not known by name, but by principles; that the Jerusalem church was a Baptist church; that the church of Antioch was a Baptist church; that all New Testament churches were Baptist churches; that

---

[29] 11.

28

whatever the scriptures [*sic.*] taught was Baptistic; that the fundamental principle of the Baptist churches was "Thus saith the Lord for everything." On this ground I stood literally; and uncompromisingly flatfooted.[30]

Given Jones' early life, it is interesting that he cannot be numbered among the progressives. Everything about the trajectory of his thought prior to 1891 suggests that his ministry would be a repudiation of the conservative position. Born December 9, 1865 in Georgia, Jones would be like many Blacks of that era who migrated from rural towns to Southern urban centers. In 1887 he arrived in Arkansas and soon united under the watch care of Centennial Baptist Church in Helena. A year later he moved to Little Rock and enrolled in Arkansas Baptist College, where he thrived in his classical and liberal arts education. His intellectual and literary gifts led to his being a popular preacher, pastor, and denominational leader. In every way, Jones was poised to ascend to national prominence within the National Baptist Convention. A prolific preacher, he was well-beloved by the Black middle class while not losing the common touch with everyday people. Both his fair complexion and insatiable intellect allowed him warm reception among noble Whites as well.

But none of this was enough for Jones. By his own account, there was a restlessness in his soul. Around 1891 he encountered Joanna Moore, a missionary with the American Baptist Missionary Society who Jones called "the sainted

---

[30] Bingham Jefferson, 30.

29

mother in Israel,"[31] who first introduced him to Holiness teaching and who prophesied to him that God was going to baptize him with the Holy Ghost. Upon hearing her message, he recalled, "Her words carried conviction. They had sweetness and power. There was no rant, no snort, no great physicality rushing about, no loud screaming, just the power that goes with clearness of vision and depth of conviction."[32] Three years later he began to experience a new work of grace in his life and ministry. Jones writes:

> In 1894 I was pastor of the Tabernacle Baptist Church of Selma, Ala., and my ministry with the church and with the Alabama Baptist ministry at large seemed to be accepted and much loved. But as I read my Bible and observed conditions, I felt that we were not, as a brother once said to me, "toting fair with Jesus." I began then to seek Him with all my heart for that power that would make my life wholly His, so that I might realize both the blessedness and usefulness of real Bible religion. I was not satisfied with a faith that brought no fruit, or else fruit of such poor quality spiritually, and a religion that none of the signs spoken of in the Bible followed. (Mark 16:14-18; Heb. 12:1-11)[33]

He later noted,

> When I first gave myself to the Lord to be sanctified,

---

[31] Weaver, C. Douglas, *Baptists and the Holy Spirit: The Contested History with Holiness-Pentecostal-Charismatic Movements*, 62.

[32] Bingham Jefferson, 24.

[33] Cobbins, 23.

(this was in 1894 at Selma) I had no idea at all of taking up holiness as a fad, or an ism, or a creed, or the slogan of a "cult." I just wanted to be personally holy. I just wished to make my own calling and election sure to my own heart by walking with God in the Spirit. As a Baptist I had doctrinal assurance; I wanted spiritual assurance, heart peace, rest of soul, the joy of salvation in the understanding of a new heart, a new mind, a new spirit, constantly renewed and comforted by the Holy Ghost. (Titus 3;5-8; John 14:15-20) But when I reached Jackson, Miss., I became convinced by the Lord that what I needed, all His people needed.[34]

In February 1895, a year after the Selma experience, Jones became pastor of Mt. Helm Baptist Church, having received a unanimous vote after turning down the call to pastor the historic church two times prior. Still viewing himself in the Baptist mainstream, he was convinced that the low spiritual state of the churches was something that should dissatisfy everyone. "In coming to Mt. Helm," writes Anita Bingham Jefferson, "he found the church and his people in general in a bad spiritual condition. He noticed especially most of his people who had been removed only thirty years from slavery had not experienced the advantages of education—religious nor secular, exposure to cultural refinement."[35] Additionally, "[Jones] found the ministers unconverted, and unreliable, proud, selfish, and even

---

[34] 23-24.

[35] Ibid., 41.

31

profligate. This grieved him."[36] Hear Jones' own words:

> But when I reached Jackson, Miss., I became
> convinced by the Lord that what I needed, all His
> people needed; that without following peace with all
> men and holiness, no man could see the Lord. Heb.
> 12:1-14; that no man could follow Christ in his own
> strength; that therefore it was the privilege and duty
> of all to be filled with the Spirit (Eph. 5:16-18) and
> walk by the Spirit (Gal. 5:15-26); that Christ in us is
> the Hope of Glory (Col. 1:27, 28), Christ the life, as
> well as Christ in Heaven the Intercessor, the High
> Priest and Advocate. Col. 1:27-29; Heb. 4:14-16.
> Christ in you, in me, in all. Christ![37]

Jones' quest for "apostolic life and power" was the
beginning of a Bapticostal renewal that took root in
Jackson.[38] "Rev. Jones did not need to trouble himself about
feeding the intellect of his people," states Bingham
Jefferson, "He sought that which was most needed—to feed
the spiritual man. His fear and love of God caused him to
offer them the "Higher Life," the VISION of Christ that he
experienced."[39] Burdened by the spiritual and moral
condition of his new assignment, Jones sought the Lord in a
six hour prayer meeting at the home of Sis Rachel Williams.
Exhausted after six hours, saying to the Lord he could pray
no more, he experienced a breakthrough:

---

[36] Ibid., 41-42.

[37] Cobbins, 24.

[38] Weaver, 62.

[39] Bingham Jefferson, 41.

Then the Lord flooded him with blessings until laughing and crying and verily kicking like an infant for holy delight, he at last begged the Lord to desist. It seemed he could stand no more, his VISION was clarified; his eyes were opened. He could see apparently the golden walls and pearly gates of the "city made without hands." Surely the heavens were open.[40]

Jones' empowerment inspired renewed leadership of both Mt. Helm and all those who would connect with his Kingdom movement. In 1897, Mt. Helm became a "temporary Jerusalem"[41] for a convention where saints could "know the Lord better and to receive *power* and *joy* for His service[.]"[42] "The sick were healed, the blind were made to see, the afflicted were blessed, and the Gospel of the New Testament was preached to the poor" during the meeting.[43] By the time conflict came to Mt. Helm over Jones's reforms, the majority (450 persons) outnumbered the detractors (150 persons) in support of the pastor and his vision. Jones insisted that what he was doing was in step with Baptist principles. For instance, "he defaulted to the Baptist insistence on the freedom of individual conscience [...] and insisted that this freedom was indispensable for following the leadership of the Holy Spirit as the New Testament

---

[40] Ibid., 42.

[41] Ibid., 51.

[42] Ibid.

[43] Ibid.

33

believers had done."[44]

Saved, Sanctified, Black and Proud: Afro-Baptist Revitalization and Decolonization

To think that Jones was simply a doctrinal extremist protesting settled Baptist doctrine is to be ignorant of history. He was seeking to remind Baptists of what they claimed. Since Baptists privilege biblical authority, Jones was convinced that his movement was in line with the New Testament. He also wanted his Spirit-empowered movement to answer the question of how the Black church would serve the holistic needs of African Americans nearing the dawn of a new century. Whereas progressives believed education and respectability were the means of this, Jones preached that all of us need more than reason. By the 1890's the quest for denominational strength eroded in some ways the centering element of spiritual vitality that was normative among Black Baptists a generation before. Williams, in *Black Baptists in Mississippi: The Tragedy of Unkept Vineyards*, rightly comments, "C.P. Jones was loved and respected, but at the time he came along, the convention (and the local Baptist church he served) was turning toward institutionalism and away from the Spirit and the Word. The zeal and fervor which had galvanized the spiritual life of Black Baptists was giving way to tradition. C. P. Jones was cast out, not because his doctrine was foreign, but because the entrenched institutional powers were organizationally complacent."[45]

To be sure, Jones was not alone in this desire to see

---

[44] Ibid., 65.

[45] 23.

34

renewed hunger for spiritual vitality among Baptists. The state convention presidency of H. W. Bowen, whose brief tenure lasted from 1894-1896, is an example. By the time he became convention president "Black Baptists in Mississippi were divided organizationally, rogue preachers and plantation churches were ignoring stewardship, doctrine and orthodoxy and white Mississippians were ready to kill any Black who threatened the political, economic and social status quo."[46] The corruption of state government was also reflected in the leadership of the convention. Though Bowen was in many respects what the progressives favored, regional denominational politics thwarted his yearnings for reform. However, his 1895 presidential address gives evidence to how the emphasis on spiritual renewal was not only the property of Jones. The final part of his message emphasized his desire for spiritual empowerment:

> I remark, in the next place, that to perform the great work that we have before us, we must be a unit, for unity is essential to success in all the undertakings in life, whether they be great or small, good or bad.

> Therefore, let us pray earnestly and unitedly that the Holy Spirit may come upon us in all His plentitude, and that He may so abide with us throughout this convention and after we have gone down from here to our respective fields of labor.

> Now let me say to you, in the last place, that unless we have the presence of the Holy Spirit to guide us

---

[46] 102.

in all we say and do, all efforts will be in vain.[47]

It is a travesty that political machinations abated Bowen's vision of a Holy Spirit-led convention that would by supernatural graces achieve great exploits in the name of the Lord Jesus Christ. It does not escape me, however, that this message was preached in the same year that Jones began his pastoral tenure at Mt. Helm. The next year, according to Jones, the General Association was held at Mt. Helm and there, along with other colleagues, he published and sold "The Work of the Holy Spirit in the Churches," a booklet length treatise expositing 1 Corinthians 12. In 1897 he hosted an interdenominational Holiness Convention at the church. "Not only were the members of [Mt. Helm] stirred and awakened but many came from other churches."[48] Between 1898 and 1901, Jones experienced greater persecution for his views and he and his cohorts were excommunicated from Baptist denominationalism. His push to change the name of Mt. Helm Missionary Baptist Church to Church of Christ, so that they would become "real historical New Testament Baptists,"[49] was indeed the lasting blow to his fellowship with Black Baptist denominational life. He was dismissed from the church in 1901 and promptly founded Christ's Tabernacle, the Mother Church of the Church of Christ (Holiness) USA, down the street from his former congregation.

Through these trials, Jones and his cohorts stood in a long line of vanguard reformers who endeavored to keep

---

[47] 105.

[48] Cobbins, 19.

[49] Ibid.

Word and Spirit in the bond of peace. I am convinced that what he was after is very much needed today. In *Pentecostal Outpourings: Revival and the Reformed Tradition*, Tom J. Nettles contends:

> Baptists survive only if they live in the mode of revival. They depend solely on conversion for the origination of church membership and upon a life of consistent holiness for its maintenance. [...] Given this abiding reality of Baptist ecclesiology, still there are times in which an extraordinary work of the Holy Spirit becomes evident. That God clearly has intentions to manifest His glory in conversion and increase of holiness at appointed seasons can hardly be denied by the observer of church history.[50]

Throughout the centuries there have been Baptists across the globe who yearned for extraordinary visitations of the Holy Spirit. For example, Vinson Synan writes, "several prominent 19th-century Baptists voiced expectations of a restoration of apostolic signs and wonders to the church."

> Such well-known Baptist leaders as C. H. Spurgeon in London and A. J. Gordon in Boston often preached about a new outpouring of the Holy Spirit in their day that would radically change the churches and the world. Indeed, Gordon, a leading turn-of-the-century Baptist pastor and teacher, is often cited as a forerunner of modern Pentecostalism because of his forceful teachings on a "baptism in the Holy Spirit" subsequent to conversion and the reality of divine

---

[50] Kindle loc. 4594.

healing in answer to prayer.[51]

Regarding Spurgeon, contemporary literature gives scant reference to his robust pneumatology, but a casual survey of his sermons and lectures clearly demonstrates that he utterly depended upon the "heavenly fire" of the Holy Spirit, which he believed to be essential to fruitful preaching and pastoral ministry.[52] In 1890, the year the regressive Mississippi Constitution discussed at the beginning of this chapter was put into law, Baptist pioneer Charles Octavious Boothe wrote *Plain Theology for Plain People*. Boothe, who pastored First Colored Baptist Church in Meridian, Mississippi, and later Dexter Avenue Baptist Church in Montgomery, Alabama, admonished:

> What wonders of power and grace may we not expect when with one accord the millions of believers in Christ throughout the world unite in earnest prayer to the God of all grace for a real Pentecostal season to be enjoyed by every nation and kindred and people and tongue under the whole heaven?[53]

That there are Baptists who search for greater usefulness to God's kingdom by seeking spiritual fullness is not as strange as some would have us to believe.

---

[51] *The Century of the Holy Spirit: 100 Years of Pentecostal and Charismatic Renewal, 1901-2001*, 186.

[52] More will be said in the concluding chapter on Spurgeon's pneumatology, especially as expounded in his Lecture XIV titled "The Holy Spirit in Connection with Our Ministry."

[53] *Plain Theology*, 88.

Conclusion

This chapter provided a sociohistorical overview of the
post-Reconstruction Black Baptist church tradition, situating
Charles Price Jones as one of several Baptist reformers in
that era providing theological and spiritual renewal
leadership for God's people wrestling with political and
social uncertainty. Its radical quality having been
unappreciated by many scholars, this research demonstrates
that Jones provided an alternative to the progressive and
conservative binary lifted up by Carter G. Woodson and his
disciples. Instead, Jones' ministry retrieved the spiritual
dynamism of previous generations of Black Baptists and
married it to biblical orthodoxy and ecumenical fellowship
in a time marked by institutionalism, denominationalism,
and corruption. Chapter three looks at ways in which Jones'
contested legacy speaks through various critical moments in
NBCUSA self-identity after him, namely, moments defined
by Martin Luther King Jr. and Paul S. Morton.

I desire to see revival and renewal in Black Baptist churches, associations, and conventions.

3

HOLY GHOST AND POWER: BLACK BAPTIST SPIRITUAL LEADERSHIP AFTER JONES

Introduction

It would seem that the Baptist denominationalists had seen the last of prophets and reformers seeking a deeper life in the Spirit following Jones' departure from Mt. Helm in 1901. Though sometimes suppressed, Jones' insistence on holy living and a more charismatic pneumatology remained impactful within the NBCUSA, its force culminating with the emergence of the Full Gospel Baptist Church Fellowship International in 1994. We would do well to learn from Jones' reforms and apply them critically today in churches not associated with Full Gospel. He "embraced the progressives' objective of making African American Christianity practical," observes David Daniels III in "The Cultural Renewal of Slave Religion: Charles Price Jones and the Emergence of the Holiness Movement in Mississippi." "Yet, he rejected the separation between what DuBois called mysticism and reason as a false dichotomy."[54] A Spirit-

---

[54] 199.

driven empowerment made this dialectic possible, and it is a beneficial expression of faith needed to address the spiritual health and social transformation concerns of this present age.

Robust Spirit language in our own time has become synonymous with the Pentecostal movment. It is important to note, however, that some of the beliefs adopted by Pentecostals cannot be ascribed to Jones, as noted in the fallout between him and Charles Harrison Mason following the latter's pilgrimage to the Azusa Revival. Jones denounced the "tongues as initial physical evidence" doctrine espoused by Charles Parham and others. "They take speaking with tongues as the evidence of the gift of the Holy Ghost," Jones states. "Now the Bible does not say this. It is a tradition of men. Add not thou to His word lest thou be found a liar."[55] In this way, Jones stands in the mainstream of contemporary Baptist thought on tongues speaking, even when such Baptists affirm its reality in the present age. Otherwise, Jones had experiences that we may classify as charismatic. He believed in the continuation of spiritual gifts and saw no contradiction between this and *Sola Scriptura*. Ever cautious of counterfeit "miracles" due in part to his stepfather's engagement in the occult, Jones nevertheless longed to see bodies healed and even raised from the dead. He did not believe that the "age of miracles" was expired. Jones opposed the Pentecostal movement as a "tongues sect" and discounted the validity of its theology and experience. However, as Daniels and others make clear, Jones was foundational in cultivating the contexts in which Charles Mason, William J. Seymour and other Black Pentecostal pioneers ultimately thrived. At the risk of hyperbole, there may not have been an Afro-Pentecostal reform movement among Baptist preachers and churches had Jones not opened

---

[55] Bingham Jefferson, 35.

hearts and minds to the Spirit's power, or been so instrumental in theological and organizational leadership. Jones could be rightfully called the father of Bapticostalism.

"Blessed Holy Spirit": Bapticostalism After Jones

As I understand it, Bapticostal identity refers to those who are convinced by the central tenets of Baptist polity and doctrine, while also affirming all the spiritual gifts discussed in 1 Corinthians 12-14 and elsewhere, and the larger spiritual orientation now associated with neo-Pentecostals: the expectancy for divine encounter. Since the Baptist part of the hybrid identity precedes the Pentecostal part, Bapticostals filter Pentecostal and Charismatic claims through the former's hermeneutic. For instance, I know very few Bapticostals who demand that every believer speak in tongues. It should be expressed, however, that Bapticostals would go further than Jones on tongues, not interpreting the gift and phenomenon quite the way he did when it became a wedge between him and Mason. I would also add that Bapticostals today need not rigidly duplicate Jones' belief on everything. But his openness to the Spirit and all the Spirit has to offer is a simple way of appreciating a Bapticostal posture. In one writing, he highlights the following:

> We were all Baptist then, the theologians had taught us that the age of miracles was past. Of course I did not believe that, because I was born again and was from the beginning a spirit-taught man. I believed the Bible. The Bible said absolutely nothing about the ages of miracles. It ascribed all possibilities to faith without saying a thing about any sort of age, it was: "If ye believer," "He that believeth", "Then that believe" (Mark 11:22-24; 16:14-18). It even

43

condemned those who did not believe.[56]

This meant Jones wasn't a cessationist. He trusted all the spiritual gifts, miracles, signs and wonders in the Bible are available to believers today. This is in stark contrast with many Baptists who believe that certain gifts and extraordinary manifestations of God's power are no longer relevant because they were meant to authenticate the Gospel prior to our having the Bible. This doctrinal divide is why 'Bapticostal' is an insufficient yet important term.

One of the most affirming moments for this was during Jerry Young's 2015 campaign for president of the NBCUSA, wherein he exclaimed, "We Baptists who have stopped by Calvary for pardon must also stop by Pentecost for power!" Though Young does not self-identify as a charismatic or Bapticostal, his use of pneumatological urgency in his presidential campaign signaled that he understood the attraction many Baptist pastors, especially younger ones, had toward movements like Full Gospel. Could this be an insinuation of a more welcoming posture toward the heirs of Jones' legacy from the convention that resisted him? Time will tell, but the nod in the direction of Bapticostals was progress, however limited. This Calvary-Pentecost continuum has a long history among Baptists but it has usually been sidelined by the more dominant cessationist wing of the fellowship. American Baptist pastor A. J. Gordon in *The Ministry of the Spirit* speaks of the need for every believer to appropriate the finished work of Pentecost in our daily lives. Resultantly, Gordon affirms

---

[56] Bingham Jefferson, 25.

We conceive that the great end for which the enduement of the Spirit is bestowed is our qualification for the highest and most effective service in the church of Christ. Other effects will certainly attend the blessing, a fixed assurance of our acceptance in Christ, and a holy separateness from the world; but these results will be conducive to the greatest and supreme end, our consecrated usefulness.[57]

Due to certain articulations of Spirit baptism doctrine, mainstream Baptists have often associated the event with salvation, thus casting it in biblically informed soteriological understanding. However, the intent of Spirit baptism as employed by Holiness and Pentecostal saints is reserved to the language of Spirit filling or Spirit fullness in Baptist circles, drawing more from Ephesians 5:8 than Acts 2. Wayne Grudem, for instance, argues that the experience Pentecostals associate with baptism of the Holy Spirit is actually a subsequent filling or refilling of the Holy Spirit.[58] Whatever biblical or theological language we use the sentiment is that we rely upon the Spirit's power for effectiveness in ministry. One hears the Spirit's conviction in Charles Spurgeon's words to preachers in the lengthy quotation below:

To us, as ministers, the Holy Spirit is absolutely essential. Without Him our office is a mere name. We claim no priesthood over and above that which

---

[57] Gordon, A. J. (1894). *The Ministry of the Spirit* (p. 74). Philadelphia: American Baptist Publication Society.

[58] He argues this in *Systematic Theology,* ch 39. Billy Graham also argues this in *The Holy Spirit: Activating God's Power in Your Life*, chs. 5, 8 and 9.

belongs to every child of God; but we are the successors of those who, in olden times, were moved of God to declare His word, to testify against transgression, and to lead His cause. Unless we have the spirit of the prophets resting upon us, the mantle which we wear is nothing but a rough garment to deceive. We ought to be driven forth with abhorrence from the society of honest men for daring to speak in the name of the Lord if the Spirit of God rests not upon us. We believe ourselves to be spokesmen for Jesus Christ, appointed to continue His witness upon earth; but upon Him and His testimony the Spirit of God always rested, and if it does not rest upon us, we are evidently not sent forth into the world as He was. At Pentecost the commencement of the great work of converting the world was with flaming tongues and a rushing mighty wind, symbols of the presence of the spirit; if, therefore, we think to succeed without the Spirit, we are not after the Pentecostal order. If we have not the Spirit which Jesus promised, we cannot perform the commission which Jesus gave.[59]

Jones embodied the "Pentecostal order" so important to fruitful ministry. But there have been other Black Baptists since him who implicitly or explicitly express the desire for Spirit-empowered ministry. From this list I lift up Martin Luther King Jr and Paul S. Morton.

Learning and Burning in the Life of Martin Luther King, Jr.

It may seem strange to some to think of how Martin

---

[59] Spurgeon's Lecture XIV: "The Holy Spirit in Connection with Our Ministry."

Luther King, Jr. is helpful in discerning how the Spirit must endue us with power from on high. Aaron J. Howard notes that though many scholars have written much about King, "the paucity of scholarship devoted to specifically examining the role of the Holy Spirit in his life and thought remains."[60] Some theologians go so far as to criticize King for himself ignoring the person, power, and working of the Spirit. But during the Montgomery bus boycott, King experienced the assurance and affirmation of the Holy Spirit in an incomparable way at the time he needed it the most. The highly intelligent and rhetorically gifted preacher arrived in Montgomery in 1954 to pastor the historic Dexter Avenue Baptist Church. He did not expect at that time that he would be thrust into public leadership so quickly when he was named the president of the Montgomery Improvement Association, which was tasked with organizing a citywide bus boycott in order to demand racially equitable treatment. Nearly a month into the boycott, the persistent death threats King received from some angry White citizens were too much to bear alone. A year later, on the verge of giving up, he sat down at his kitchen table the night of January 27, 1956, and bowing over a cup of coffee began to pray aloud for divine assistance. In that moment of desperation King relates

> I experienced the presence of the Divine as I had never experienced Him before. It seemed as though I could hear the quiet assurance of an inner voice saying, "Stand up for righteousness, stand up for truth; and God will be at your side forever." Almost

---

[60] Howard, "The Manifestation of an Immanent God: The Holy Spirit in the Theology of Martin Luther King Jr.," *Revives My Soul Again: The Spirituality of Martin Luther King Jr.*, 91.

at once my fears began to go. My uncertainty
disappeared. I was ready to face anything.[61]

This mystical experience, often overlooked by those wanting
to emulate King's public theological leadership, can be seen
as a work of the Holy Spirit, though he does not reference it
as such. But it is significant that this third-generation Baptist
pastor speaks about never before experiencing anything as
moving in his ministry as that experience. David Garrow
asserts that the kitchen experience "was the most important
night of his life."[62] That night religion became real to the
then 27-year-old man of God in a way that his early
childhood conversion or seminary education had not
facilitated. Much like Jones before him, he came to know
that intellect and natural gifting would not suffice for the
daunting challenges ahead of him. King needed what so
many everyday Baptists intuit: a religion he could feel. As
with Jones' Selma experience, King's Montgomery
experience changed the trajectory of his life and bequeathed
to him the "learning and burning" foundational for vanguard
prophetic leadership then and today. King's dialectical
approach to the pietistic and protest traditions of the Black
church gave witness to a reconciled awareness of the Spirit's
work in and through the church for the salvation of the
world. It is a cohesiveness that we must hold on to for future
generations.

To call King a charismatic would be suspect, however.
His kitchen table experience seems to be the exception and
not the rule of his ministry. This doesn't mean, however, that

---

[61] King, *Stride Toward Freed*, pp 133-135.

[62] Raphael G. Warnock, *The Divided Mind of the Black Church: Theology, Piety, and Public Witness,* 39.

awareness of the Spirit was absent from his service. Howard asserts that King's book *Stride toward Freedom* "can best be interpreted as a pnumatological narrative wherein King comes to terms with a newfound relationship with the Holy Spirit and experiences the concominant realization that this same Spirit quickens history through ecstatic intervention."[63] More could be read into the setting of King's last sermon prior to his assassination, then. Respectable, polished, and quintessentially middle class, King represented the highest aspirations of the progressive reformers discussed in previous chapters. But the night of April 3, 1968, the consummate dignified Baptist stood to preach in the pulpit of Charles Harrison Mason Temple Church of God in Christ in Memphis, Tennessee, an edifice memorializing the Afro-Pentecostal pioneer anathematized by his Baptists colleagues. Behind King hung a large banner that read "Growth and Progress" with Zechariah 4:6 emblazoned below those words: "Not by might, nor by power, but by My Spirit saith the Lord of hosts." Tired and mentally preoccupied, the golden voice of the Civil Rights Movement preached hope to hundreds of poor Memphians who sat in solidarity with sanitation workers striking for just labor. His "I've Been to the Mountaintop" sermon riveted the congregation as his poetic words crescendoed toward the conclusion. Like Moses he talked about seeing a God-inspired vision of the Promised Land.

Well, I don't know what will happen now. We've got some difficult days ahead. But it really doesn't matter with me now, because I've been to the mountaintop.

---

[63] Howard, 102.

And I don't mind.

Like anybody, I would like to live a long life.
Longevity has its place. But I'm not concerned about
that now. I just want to do God's will. And He's
allowed me to go up to the mountain. And I've looked
over. And I've seen the Promised Land. I may not get
there with you. But I want you to know tonight, that
we, as a people, will get to the promised land![64]

Not much has been written that identifies the
pneumatological connections between these events. Even
more, the connection between what God was doing in the
Civil Rights Movement and the Charismatic renewal of
mainline white churches in the 1960s "should have been
made, but never has been made," according to Ithiel
Clemmons.[65] To be sure, it has not really been made with
those in the Black church tradition until more recently. This
is because though the Holy Spirit gets honorable mention,
many Christians in the West have disenchanted theological
imaginations given to them by modernity. Within the last
few decades there has been a renaissance in pneumatology
that thankfully corrects the blind spot. "The rise of the
charismatic movement within virtually every mainstream
church," writes Alister McGrath, "has ensured that the Holy
Spirit figures prominently on the theological agenda."[66] This
is true for the National Baptist family, but more research

---

[64] King, Martin Luther. *I've Been to the Mountaintop*, 1994.

[65] Yong, Amos. *The Spirit Poured Out on All Flesh: Pentecostalism and the
Possibility of Global Theology*, 79.

[66] Karkkainen, Veli-Matti, *Pneumatology: The Holy Spirit in Ecumenical,
International, and Contextual Perspective*. 10.

must be done to quantify the impact neo-Pentecostalism has had on the largest Black denominational fellowship.

As a corollary to this, we must look to another case study found in the African Methodist Episcopal Church context, as no official study on neo-Pentecostalism and the NBCUSA has been published at the time of this composition. C. Eric Lincoln and Lawrence H. Mamiya detail this in *The Black Church in the African American Experience*. Unlike the sociological distinctions noted between Black church progressives and conservatives generations ago, Lincoln and Mamiya attest: "The membership of most of these neo-Pentecostal churches consists of a mix of a middle-income working-class and middle-class blacks, [...] and some of the Black urban poor, the latter tending to be attracted by the informal, less structured, and highly spirited worship services."[67] Moreover, these "Methocostal" churches converge "deep Pentecostal piety and the A.M.E. tradition of involvement in progressive politics and political activism." Like Jones and his ecclesiological vision, these churches and their leaders choose the best from both the progressive and conservative traditions, creating an altogether new phenomenon that mediates between the two. Pastorally, most of the neo-Pentecostal A.M.E.'s were seminary trained and to varying degrees involved in the Civil Rights Movement. Lincoln and Mamiya note, "Some of these activists felt burned out by the continuous struggle and sought a deeper, spiritual side."[68] In some sense, King standing in the Mason Temple's pulpit becomes a signpost of a Bapticostal hope for learning and burning as it applies

---

[67] 386.

[68] Ibid., 387.

to the quest for social justice and desire for spiritual gifts.

Beyond False Choices: The Full Gospel Baptist Church Fellowship and Black Baptist Identities

Though King didn't call himself a Bapticostal, we can intuit him as a bridge between Jones and the Full Gospel Baptist movement that followed decades later. Like Jones, King, a young pastor-scholar, was no longer welcome in the NBC and co-founded the Progressive National Baptist Convntion in 1961.

It is clear from the emergence of the Full Gospel Baptist Church Fellowship International that a current of charismatic spirituality surged throughout the what remained of convention for decades. Founded in 1994 by Paul S. Morton, Full Gospel has grown to be a highly visible reformation of Black Baptist charismatics. According to Morton in his autobiography, in 1992 he preached for the NBCUSA annual session. Members of the platform and audience jested about Morton's recent neo-Pentecostal church innovations and it was at this meeting that he felt God releasing him to start a new work. But his sermon was electrifying and the audience erupted in unrestrained praise for a considerable duration of time. Following the message, convention president T. J. Jemison exclaimed, "Paul, you've got something like I've never seen before. These people love you. Listen to them. They can't stop them. When you preach [...] you've got 'presence.'" Morton retorted, "No, Mr. President; it's called 'the anointing!'" "Call it whatever you want. You've got it!"[69] Though Morton contends he was being groomed by Jemison to succeed him as convention

---

[69] *Changing Forward: Experiencing God's Unlimited Power*, Kindle loc. 1100.

president, that annual session provided Morton with clarity about his future. Two years later, Morton would go on to host the first Full Gospel Fellowship meeting; approximately 30,000 persons attended the gathering hosted in the New Orleans Superdome. Morris and Lee recount the reflections of one Baptist pastor:

> It began because there has always existed in the Baptist communion those with an appetite for a more spiritual, demonstrative type of worship style. Historically those individuals have been heavily influenced by the Pentecostal tradition and yet have remained within the Baptist communion and in many respects the worship style has been stifled in the Baptist witness. So Bishop Morton really tapped into kind of a sleeping giant in terms of the vastness that really wanted to move in that particular direction.[70]

Despite this, Full Gospel's popularity was met with suspicion and dismissiveness. Many NBC leaders silently requested that those in Morton's movement resign from their convention appointments. The inclusion of episcopal leadership alarmed classical Baptists concerned that Full Gospel was more Pentecostal than Baptist and would ultimately inflict harm on "sound" Baptist doctrine. Still, others laughed off Morton and Full Gospel and said it was a fad that would be soon wither away. A quarter of a century later, Full Gospel is still viable. In 2015 Morton willingly stepped down from his International Presiding Bishop position and Joseph W. Walker III of Nashville, TN, was

---

[70] Aldon D. Morris and Shayne Lee, "The National Baptist Convention: Traditions and Contemporary Challenges," in Roozen and Nieman (eds), *Church, Identity and Change: Theology and Denominational Structures in Unsettled Times*, 370.

named his successor. Since that time, Walker has aggressively broadened Full Gospel's reach. Whereas Morton was more of a pioneer in bridging the theological and liturgical gaps between Baptists and Pentecostals, Walker has done more in his tenure to convince skeptics that Full Gospel is serious about intellectual discourse, social justice advocacy, and philanthropy. Walker travels the nation preaching in major mainstream Baptist pulpits, like Ebenezer Baptist Church, where Martin Luther King, Jr., once co-pastored with his father. In ways more demonstrable than Morton, Walker illustrates the *via media* that Jones operated within, being a graduate of Vanderbilt Divinity School and Princeton Theological Seminary. His intellect matches his spiritual acumen, and his wide-ranging network makes him unique among neo-Pentecostal Baptists.

Gifts and the Gospel

So far, NBCUSA has not made any official statements affirming or condemning Full Gospel. H. Beecher Hicks, a National Baptist pastor, wrote affirmatively about Full Gospel two decades ago. "This Fellowship is not designed to threaten or replace mainline denominations, but to provide an opportunity for those who wanted to remain Baptist and yet exercise all of the gifts of the Spirit, particularly speaking in tongues."[71] Though generally ridiculed at its inception, there are growing numbers in those ranks that possess views similar to Hicks'.

Though more research is necessary, anecdotally we can

---

[71] H. Beecher Hicks, "Challenge to the African American Church: Problems and Perspectives for the Third Millennium," Journal of Religious Thought 51 (1994), 81-97.

surmise that Full Gospel has had a major, positive impact on Black Baptist pastoral identity for those within and outside that movement increasingly unapologetic about their choosing to be Baptist and charismatic. What we see is the rise in the number of Baptists who readily embrace theological positions once considered beyond the pale of Baptist doctrine. They may have concerns about Baptist bishops, but don't see much harm in the trend because most Full Gospel churches still maintain local autonomy, an essential doctrine for classical Baptists. Also, cessationism is not as predominant as it was a generation ago, with younger Baptist pastors seeing that argument as deeply flawed; in turn they are either cautiously continuationists (believing all spiritual gifts are for the Church today but must be used in the strictest obedience to Pauline restrictions) or full-blown charismatics. Our Southern Baptist cousins have done a better job documenting their charismatic resurgence. A 1997 study by "LifeWay Research on the use of private prayer language indicates that half of Southern Baptist pastors believe the Holy Spirit gives some people a special language to pray to God."[72] In 2015, the SBC's International Mission Board dropped its ban on tongues-speech.[73] Sam Storms, John Piper, Wayne Grudem, and Gregg R. Allison are charismatic pastor-theologians beloved by Southern Baptists and their writings and preachments have gone a long way in helping them ponder anew the workings and gifts of the Holy Spirit.

But National Baptists have not been as forward with

---

[72] Lovelace, Libby, "LifeWay releases prayer language study." Baptist Press. http://www.bpnews.net/25765/lifeway-releases-prayer-language-study

[73] Smietana, Bob. "International Mission Board Drops Ban on Speaking in Tongues. Christianity Today. http://www.christianitytoday.com/ct/2015/may-web-only/imb-ban-speaking-in-tongues-baptism-baptist-missionary.html

their thoughts in writing. However, there are serious and important criticisms that have been verbalized, one of them being that the gifts shouldn't be equated with the Gospel. The language "Full Gospel" implies to some that other Baptists have an incomplete gospel, an implication based on the fact that those Baptists aren't tongue talking, hand laying, prophesying sorts. Indeed, if this is what is meant by "full gospel" then the criticism holds. The Gospel is the life, crucifixion, burial, and resurrection of Jesus Christ. The Gospel is a Person, the Lord and Savior of the world. Nowhere in Scripture are spiritual gifts elevated to that place. But I should add that I have yet to meet any charismatic Baptist who says the gifts are equated with the Gospel. In fact, more of them I know are trying to make sense of what they see in the Bible and have experienced in relation to their imbedded theology.

I have taught numerous times in the General Missionary Baptist State Convention of Mississippi and have discovered that a host of Missionary Baptists in this state secretly are continuationists or charismatics. This could be due to FBGCF or the saturation of religious broadcasting and Gospel music with neo-Pentecostal sensibilities. In many cases, however, I have heard from Missionary Baptists whose plain reading of the Bible led them to embrace all spiritual gifts as a doctrinal option, or they have witnessed or experienced these gifts themselves. They share this in private conversations, not wanting to be shunned by traditionalists among them. With or without the movement founded to give Baptists the right to choose, there are many Baptists today who are much more open to the surprising movements of the Holy Spirit and seek to glorify Jesus and share His Gospel in all the Spirit's fullness. Now is a good time for them to be free to choose without feeling forced to leave their native contexts. Moreover, many of us are now called to revive and reform those very settings.

Contemporary Promises and Perils of Bapticostal Identity

Thus far, I have charted the ways in which pneumatological discourse and influences have shaped, challenged, and compelled fresh notions of Black Baptist identity. From Charles Jones to Martin Luther King, Jr., to Joseph Warren Walker III, we see that experiences of divine empowerment have been essential to cultivating vanguard movement leaders whose witnesses are global in scope and transgenerational in impact. Whatever else can be said about the Baptist retrieval of charismatic pneumatology, this much is true: as we move further into the third millennium, a robust Spirit-empowered model of Black Baptist pastoral identity must be mainstreamed in both traditional churches and reformations that come alongside them. King's ministry utilized the Hegelian dialectic, by which the preacher and prophet synthesized seemingly disparate positions into fresh perspectives on spirituality, service, and social justice. What will be borne out more in the final chapter is how a dialectical approach to what Raphael Warnock calls the "divided mind of the Black church" resolves this assumed disunity in thought and praxis. Speaking about the general Black church tradition, Larry Murphy writes, "Piety was not one thing and liberation its antithesis. Rather, the latter derived its motive power and its transcendent validation from the former."[74] Instead of the binary theo-logic of many Western Christians, at its best the Black church tradition incorporates a holistic spirituality that enlivens our interiority as well as social transformation. In the shadows

---

[74] Warnock, 37.

of King's public leadership is mystic Howard Thurman who called his mentees to genuine authenticity through the cultivation of their spiritual senses. King's leadership would have lacked something special without the mystical dimension.

The National Baptist Convention and her churches are long overdue for a public and non-punitive discussion about the role of the Holy Spirit in our ministries beyond the necessary reality of salvation and sealing. Certainly, we Baptists are well aware of the finished work of the cross and how saving grace is imparted to us by the Spirit. We even note the work of the Holy Spirit in effective preaching, shouting, "Help me Holy Ghost!" and "I feel my help!" in enthusiastic preaching moments. What is less defined is how the Spirit continues to anoint and gift the church for effective ministry and how that effectiveness is not always pragmatic but always is spiritually discerned. Thankfully, growing numbers of Baptists have been unashamed in their emphasis on the whole scope of the Spirit's work.

Regarding church growth, social justice advocacy, spiritual formation and discipleship training, and other ministerial efforts, many are now coming to terms with the end of their power and the efficacy of spiritual empowerment. In *Jesus, Continued...: Why the Spirit Inside You is Better than Jesus Beside You*, J.D. Greear remarks that Leslie Newbigin points out the "dynamic operation of the Holy Spirit" is what made the qualitative difference in the first-century church despite being "by our standards, poorly staffed, poorly resourced, poorly equipped, and in an extremely hostile, emphatically pluralistic culture."[75]

---

[75] Greear, 143.

Reemphasizing the pneumatological dimension of ministry effectiveness is crucial for us as we go deeper into the third millennium. Out of better teaching or shear desperation, a new generation of Baptists, some still related to the NBCUSA, is trusting less in their might and more in the Spirit's power. The future of Black church leadership, of pastor-theologians in particular, must take seriously the "learning and burning" and "piety and protest" dimensions of a liberating faith enabled by the Spirit for reformative and transformative work in the church and in the world.

A Mississippi pastor I know is a case in point. Though a Baby Boomer, he is very well suited for this present age of spiritual renewal. Like many Black Baptists, Robert McCallum grew up in a relatively traditional Missionary Baptist church, but it was not until his mid-20's that an encounter with the living Christ became real and relevant in his life. What the Lord did in him caused him to drink from multiple Christian fountains and he would come to experience God in Christ in a powerful way at a charismatic church in his native Jackson. It was there he first learned about and experienced various gifts of the Spirit never discussed in his Baptist upbringing. McCallum's brother-in-law, who at the time was a staunch Baptist, thought he and his sister had joined a cult. Concerned for his family's safety, this pastor's brother-in-law attended a meeting or two and his suspicion gave way to surrender. Interestingly, following that encounter he went on to leave the Baptist tradition and founded an independent charismatic ministry that is one of Jackson's largest and influential churches, while my other pastor friend remains an influential leader in the Baptist fold.

Still a Missionary Baptist, McCallum's life and ministry were no longer the same after his charismatic experience. The emphasis on the Holy Spirit animated his preaching and leadership. Wanting more learning with his burning, he enrolled in the Master of Divinity program at Reformed Theological Seminary (RTS), a cessationist school. There he came to be known affectionately as the "Reformed Baptist Charismaniac." Fellow seminarians and professors joked that RTS was all Word and no Spirit, and that the Black church was all Spirit and no Word. Though this is a stereotype of a more complicated reality, the bourgeoning Bapticostal was seen as synthesizing the Spirit and the Word traditions dialectically. He saw this as the biblical way. Over the years he has touched thousands as a pastor, teacher, seminary instructor, and leader in the state convention. He insists that more of us must preach and teach on our reliance upon the Holy Spirit in our churches and ministries. "Too much of what goes for effective ministry," McCallum has said, "is born out of perspiration, not inspiration. We Baptists have forsaken certain biblical language and practices to avoid being confused with Pentecostals."

This Baby Boomer pastor represents on the local and state levels critical support for a more Spirit-driven ministry. There are signs of hope in the NBCUSA, as well. Alyn E. Waller, pastor of the Enon Tabernacle Baptist Church in Philadelphia, PA, and a past president of Lott Carey Convention, confessed during a lecture at a NBC meeting that though he has no desire to join FGBCFI he affirmed all the gifts of the Spirit. In a transformational encounter with God, Waller experienced the Spirit convicting him of sin followed by a "move of God" that resulted in the "charismatic experience" of tongues speaking. Waller saw no discrepancy between his tongues speech and Baptist fidelity. A generation ago, Morton was given an ultimatum that pushed him out. But according to the NBC website,

Waller "gave a thought-provoking, critical lecture."[76]Waller was unapologetic about his stance and shared it before hundreds of pastors and ranking members of the denomination's leadership. As research above demonstrates, much has changed since 1890 or even 1990. It is time for the NBCUSA and other Baptist fellowships to take seriously publicly addressing the matter.

When King delivered his last sermon on the eve of his assassination, it may not have dawned on him that he was speaking in the pulpit of a church named in honor of a Baptist reformer turned Pentecostal apostle. The groundbreaking spiritual work Mason and Jones offered throughout the deep South was long seen as ancillary to the social gospeling of progressive Baptists. Calvin White injects, "Mainstream Black religious denominations such as the Baptists and Methodists accused Mason and Jones of retarding the efforts of self-help, racial uplift, and respectability, thus rendering them and the emerging Black Holiness movement pariahs[.]"[77] By King's youthful admission, he was judgmental toward what he considered the emotionalism of his fundamentalist Baptist upbringing and that of the Holiness-Pentecostal traditions that sprang from it. He had a change of mind, however, as he moved deeper into the Civil Rights Movement and saw that the religious expressions and visions of "the least of these" had inestimable value. In fact, King preached at Mason Temple

---

[76] Alyn Waller, "A Conversation on Church Growth and the Millennial Generation," National Baptist Convention USA Mid-Winter Board Meeting, January 10, 2017. http://www.nationalbaptist.com/resources/sermons/index.html

[77] White, Jr., Calvin. "In the Beginning, There Stood Two: Arkansas Roots of the Black Holiness Movement," The Arkansas Historical Quarterly, vol. LXVIII, no. 1, Spring 2009.

COGIC before on March 18, 1968. According to White, more than nine thousand filled the sanctuary and spilled out into the temple grounds to hear the Baptist preacher. White writes,

> In a speech lasting a little over an hour, King stated, "We have Baptists, Methodists, Episcopalians, Presbyterians, and members of the Church of God in Christ, we are all together." As he ended his speech, he argued that blacks must unite beyond class lines and explained, "The Negro 'haves' must join hands with the Negro 'have-nots' in this fight."[78]

This fusion politics was punctuated when King returned to Memphis and Mason Temple for his April 3 address to the sanitation workers' strike supporters. White continues, "On that night, King, the embodiment of the cult of respectability, looked into the waiting eyes of a crowd composed of a large number of COGIC members. Finally, the Black middle class had found common cause with the Church of God in Christ that transcended class and religious differences—the basic dignity of man."[79]

Conclusion

Following the controversial ministry of Charles Price Jones, at least two other major tensions happened in NBCUSA life with the rise of Martin Luther King and his nonviolent resistance to injustice, and the emergence of the

---

[78] White, 128

[79] Ibid., 129

Paul Morton's Full Gospel movement. Implicit in all three moments is a question regarding the Holy Spirit and leadership. Said differently, the question is about how should we envision our calling in light of systemic challenges in both church and society. The potential for unity across class, doctrinal, and generational lines resides in every vanguard movement this work lifts up. From the Holiness revival in the 1890's, to the Civil Rights revival of the 1960's, to the Bapticostal renewal of the 1990's, there are rich resources for Christ-centered, Spirit-empowered ecumenism within and beyond the Black church. This chapter attempted to demonstrate this. Chapter four will go further in developing a model based on these insights.

Anointed preaching and leadership are ultimately about maintaining the spiritual nature of our service.

4

WORD AND SPIRIT BAPTISTS: RENEWING THE BAPTIST VANGAURD

Introduction

R. T. Kendall, in *"Word Spirit Power: What Happens When You Seek All God Has to Offer,"* offers the following:

> A silent divorce has taken place in the Church, generally speaking, between the Word and the Spirit. And when there is a divorce, sometimes the children stay with the mother, sometimes with the father. In this divorce, we have those on the "Word" side and those on the "Spirit" side. Those who go to "Word" churches do not expect to *see* much; they go to hear. "Thank you for your word," is a typical comment to the preacher following the sermon. When people go to "Spirit" churches, they usually do not expect to *hear* much; they go to see.

> But when the two are brought together, the simultaneous combination will mean spontaneous combustion. The day will come--and I believe it is at hand--when, as my friend Lyndon Bowring put it,

those who come to see will hear and those who come to hear will see.[80]

In the preceding chapters, I provided historical and contemporary contextualization for this case study. This chapter puts forth the beginnings of a Word and Spirit model for Holy Spirit-empowered ministry and revival in Baptist churches.

Baptist Renewal and Controversies

"The challenge to the Black Baptist Church in Mississippi," writes John H. Williams, Jr., "is to renew its initial religious heritage contribution and adapt that contribution to meet community needs."[81] These words, published in 1992, are even more relevant today. Black Baptists in Mississippi and beyond journeying further into the third millennium desire in greater numbers Holy Spirit-empowered ecclesial visions for the contemporary age. Unfortunately, the desire for reform and renewal in our churches has not always been met with corresponding action. As in previous generations, however, servant leadership is required. The kind of leadership required for the task before us, that of renewing the church for the sake of the world, is not to be found in word or even deed only. Paul writes in 1 Corinthians 2:4 that we need leaders who are not simply eloquent or effective, but who lead "in demonstration of the Spirit and of power." Far too many pastors today turn to pragmatic models taken from secular business culture in order to divine spiritual things. To be

---

[80] 43.

[81] *Black Baptists in Mississippi: A Historical Perspective*, 82.

66

sure, there is much we can learn from the resources outside the church, but these lessons should simply supplement, not substitute, deeper wells of wisdom that can only be accessed through the presence and power of the Holy Spirit. We are captivated by what Skye Jethani calls "Church, Inc.," which he defines as "shorthand for ministry devoid of mystery, for pastors who assume that the exercise of their calling is a matter of skill more than the gravity of their soul. It represents the exchange for transcendent calling of Christian ministry with mere management of religious institutions and services."[82] From this captivity we must be delivered if Black Baptist churches will be of any earthly good in the years to come.

Jones' renewal movement was an exciting one amid the varieties of post-Reconstruction Black religious transformation, and one that survived him in myriad ways. Without Jones, we could not have the Church of Christ (Holiness) USA, the Church of God in Christ, particular streams of Pentecostalism, rich deposits of sacred hymnody, and so on. He was the spiritual father for these movements and though some of them differ with him on finer distinctives, a genealogical connection nevertheless remains. More importantly, I contend that Jones is central to retrieving for Black Baptists a spiritual leadership model. Specifically bringing Jones out of the shadows and among his native Baptists may be questionable to some. Denominationalism has caused some Baptists to build walls of hostility instead of bridges of understanding. This is certainly true for other notable Baptists who were generous

---

[82] *Immeasurable: Reflections on the Soul of Ministry in the Age of Church, Inc.*, 9.

in their orthodoxy. In 1859 the Columbia Baptist Association in South Carolina called Spurgeon a "semi-Baptist" for his open communion views. The same year, and for the same reason, Joseph Walker (not to be confused with the bishop of Full Gospel), the editor of Georgia's Baptist Champion, judged that Baptists could not recognize Spurgeon as a "sound Baptist preacher." A writer to North Carolina's Biblical Record in the same manner argued that "Spurgeon is a great man but no Baptist." Joseph Otis, editor of Kentucky Baptists' Western Recorder, did not consider Spurgeon a Baptist at all in 1860.[83]

Undoubtedly, Spurgeon, once characterized by American Baptists as being outside the Baptist communion, is now celebrated in the United States as one of the world's greatest Baptist preachers and pastors. A new generation of preachers have discovered his eloquent exposition of Scripture and model it. There are even now Spurgeon study Bibles, daily devotionals, and other texts populating Baptist and Evangelical bookshelves. In much the same way predominantly White Baptists in our age have embraced Spurgeon, I am inviting this generation of Black Baptists to do the same for Jones. A gifted expositor, hymnist, organizer, Jones provides for us a fresh model for pastoral leadership not grounded in secular pragmatism. His is the constant reminder than any lasting personal and social transformation is utterly dependent upon God's Holy Spirit.

I offer a caveat here. Focusing on Jones runs the risk of elevating a "great man" myth that can turn this historic figure

---

[83] Gregory A. Wills, "The Ecclesiology of Charles H. Spurgeon: Unity, Orthodoxy, and Denominational Identity", Midwestern Journal of Theology, Fall 2015, vol. 14, no. 2., 50. (http://s3.amazonaws.com/mbts-mediafolder/wp-content/uploads/2013/03/25145502/FA15_MJT_Final.pdf)

into a kind of idol to whom we look nostalgically. But this is not the point. Rather, Jones is an icon through which we gaze upon the Triune God at work in the world. Any disciple of Jesus Christ can do the great exploits Jones and his cohorts did if he or she is surrendered. Jesus said, "Truly, truly, I say to you, whoever believes in me will also do the works that I do; and greater works than these will he do, because I am going to the Father. Whatever you ask in my name, this I will do, that the Father may be glorified in the Son." (John 14:12-13 ESV)

The Anointing Makes the Difference

"The anointing" has become the common parlance to speak to the kind of empowerment we seek in order to do great exploits for the Kingdom. Indeed, to be *Christian* is to be anointed (Romans 8:9). 1 John 2:20 says, "[…] you have an anointing from the Holy One, and all you know the truth." (NIV) In that sense, all followers of Jesus are anointed. But the nomenclature points to the distinguishing element that separates what preachers and pastors do from other forms of speech-making and leadership. We are not stand-up comics, motivational speakers, or CEOs of Fortune 500 companies. We are ambassadors of the Kingdom, heralds of the Gospel, stewards of mysteries. When I speak of anointing, I think specifically about Jesus' ministry manifesto in Luke 4:18-19 where he says, "The Spirit of the Lord is upon me, because he has anointed me to proclaim good news to the poor." (ESV) Jesus testifies to having an anointing that gave him clear focus, purpose, and passion. Our singing, preaching, praying, and prophesying are enhanced by supernatural power, the power of the Holy Spirit, when we are anointed. As Joseph W. Walker III defines it, "[t]he anointing empowers us with supernatural strength to do what we could never do in our natural state."[84] This supernatural strength, then, produces unusual results, as Steven Headrick notes. "While unusual in human terms," he says, "these effects should be typical of the Christian's anointed life."[85] Particularly speaking to the element of spiritual empowerment, William C. Turner argues that "[s]uch empowerment from above enabled one to stand over against the world. [...] Despite calamity, suffering, and hostile culture, there is access to power from this spiritual realm, which provides toughness, resilience, inner fortitude, and endurance to defy odds of every sort.[86]

Anointed preaching and leadership are ultimately about maintaining the spiritual nature of our service. Geoffrey Gunns states, "Spiritual leaders are men and women who have been called by God to lead His people; who have been filled and empowered by the Holy Spirit; and who have submitted to His will in all that they do and say."[87] Because the Holy Spirit, and not we ourselves, has made us overseers (Acts 20:28), we must constantly rely upon the Holy Spirit and, as William H. Willimon notes, understand our office and authority "both as a gift of an effusive Spirit and as the designation of the Spirit-filled community."[88] Though it

---

[84] *Leadershifts: Mastering Transitions in Leadership and Life*, 67.

[85] Headrick, "A Case Study Examining Growth in Understanding Biblical Anointing at Faith Baptist Church," 34.

[86] *The United Holy Church of America*, 124.

[87] *Spiritual Leadership: A Guide to Developing Spiritual Leaders in the Church*, 68.

[88] *Pastor: The Theology and Practice of Ordained Ministry*, 37.

cannot be denied that pastors must attend to technical, practical, and pragmatic matters of leadership, spiritual leaders must contend that "[m]inistry is also charismatic, something that God gives and demands. Leadership in the church is an institution, but it begins as an event. If God should withdraw this gift, then ministry would collapse and all efforts to make ministry make sense, apart from the gifts of the Holy Spirit, would be futile."[89]

From Professionalization to Pentecostalization

John Piper's book *Brothers, We are Not Professionals* opens with this sobering rebuke: "We pastors are being killed by the professionalizing of the pastoral ministry."[90] For particular reasons, the Black Baptist pastorate following slavery wrestled with the ideals of professionalization. The progressives were, by and large, committed to a professional ministry occupied by learned men of impeccable moral respectability. That way, they assumed, Black Baptist pastors would be taken seriously by their Methodist counterparts and genteel White society. In more recent years, a similar insecurity about the pastorate exists, for similar and different reasons. Nostalgically, many Black pastors remember when they were the center of the community's aspirations. As WEB DuBois mentioned, the Black preacher was everything to the Black community. Following the social advancements resulting from the Civil Rights Movement, the Black preacher was marginalized by the Black politician, the Black athlete, and the Black entertainer.

---

[89] Ibid.

[90] Piper, 1.

Secular rappers, not sacred rhetoricians, became the prophets of a new generation dealing with the anxiety that came with the complicated successes and failures of a desegregated society. As urban cities and rural towns across America remained in generational poverty, Hip Hop culture demanded that Black youth "fight the power." When rap was mainstreamed, youth were in turn told to acquiesce to crass materialism and the sexual objectification of women. Black preachers, sidelined by this new mood, were seen as irrelevant. Even more, they became the laughing stock of civil society due to cinematic and literary representations of them as pimps, hustlers, and con-artists.

Late modernity has brought with it some good news, interestingly. As Jason E. Vickers states in *Minding the Good Ground: A Theology for Church Renewal*, "We realize that our preoccupation with the professionalization of the ministry may have had more to do with our desire for intellectual and cultural respectability than with our desire for things of God."[91] The necessary turn away from professionalization requires a return to a more robust pneumatology. What our times demand is the *pentecostalization* of the church, by which I mean the reemphasizing of the outpouring of the Holy Spirit at Pentecost and by whose constant indwelling the church subsists. It is another way of echoing Jerry Young's claim that Baptists must go to Pentecost for our power. As Vickers eloquently offers, "From its inception, the church has been and is a charismatic community whose life depends entirely on the presence and power of the Holy Spirit, through whom and by whom the church does everything that she does, including proclaiming the good news about the life, death,

---

[91] Vickers, 9.

and resurrection of Jesus; assisting persons in repentance for sin; catechizing and baptizing new converts; praying and worshipping together; freely sharing resources within and without the community; and breaking bread together."[92] Every element of the church's witness to Christ is infused with the Spirit's presence. Hence, we must not only call Baptist pastors to perform spiritual practices, but to acknowledge the life in the Spirit.[93] "Although today's churches are separated in time, culture, and distance from the primitive church," write the Study and Research Division of the Baptist World Alliance, "our need for reliance upon God's Spirit is much the same."[94]

Living in and keeping step with the Spirit, Bapticostals are poised to make critical impact in our times. Ours is a time that necessitates pastors who are spiritual, ethical, and transformative; pastors who are on the front lines of struggle and sanctification of souls and societies. We need anointed leaders like Charles Price Jones who will be led and full of the Holy Spirit in order to do great exploits in the name of Jesus Christ.

Conclusion: To the Sons and Daughters of Africa

Charles Price Jones was a renaissance man. A visionary church planter, hymnologist, institution builder, and pastor-theologian, Jones was graced to bring spiritual and social reform to the Black community following the years of

---

[92] Vickers, 36.

[93] See Gordon Fee's chapter in *Life in the Spirit: Spiritual Formation in Theological Perspective* (ed. Jeffrey P. Greenman and George Kalantzis).

[94] *We Baptists,* Kindle loc. 1648.

Reconstruction and into dawn of the modern Civil Rights Movement. This he initially did as a young man, only in his early 30's when he arrived to Jackson to pastor Mt. Helm. His intellect, oratory, youthful zeal, and refinement were no match for the sanctifying power of the Holy Spirit that consumed his thoughts and deeds. Unapologetic about his Blackness, he worked among the sons and daughters of Africa with unyielding joy even when persecuted by them. Unashamed of the Gospel, he preached Christ and him crucified above every philosophy of human origin. God commenced Jones' work when he was a relatively young man, demonstrating how God does not despise youth in kingdom work, and God continues to call and empower many young leaders among us today.

Based on the above-mentioned qualities, I submit that we learn from Jones that leaders today are young, or young at heart, visionaries who see Christ glorified in individuals and institutions in ways not yet actualized by the status quo. These young leaders employ their intellects, creativity, vast networks, and passionate service in the work of the Lord and in the power of God. They know that their mission and success rely not on their power alone, but more in the grace and anointing of the Holy Spirit. They approach social issues first as spiritual leaders, discerning the actual "powers that be" behind the flesh and blood figures that may resist church change and social uplift.

5

WHERE DO WE GO FROM HERE?

This book began as a frustration. As a Christian who chooses to be Baptist by conviction, I found it strange that so many of my colleagues were reticent about acknowledging out loud their hunger for deeper spiritual insight and power. This reservation, in many instances, has come from younger pastors who want to remain loyal to their pastoral mentors and not to alienate themselves from their congregations or conventions. We rightly shy away from the prosperity prophecies and money lines we see on The Word Network or TBN, and all of the other excesses stereotypical in some charismatic circles, but as I attempt to show in this book, there are large numbers of Black Baptists who espouse beliefs about the Holy Spirit and spiritual empowerment that are, in many instances, mainstream affirmations. From this we should uphold the place of charismatic Baptist identity within historic churches and conventions, recognizing that it need not be in conflict with broader understandings of Baptist polity and doctrine. Furthermore, now is the time for thoughtful and critical engagement of this Bapticostal approach to life and leadership, so that we do not continue to be seduced by the trendy things that pass for ministerial strategy today. I believe Bapticostalism, as I have defined it, is a way forward with integrity. With learning and burning, piety and protest, Word and Spirit, this vanguard of Bapticostal reformers may indeed be the answer to the missional drift, institutional decline, social disintegration, and spiritual apathy so prominent across the Afro-Baptist landscape.

I am grateful to pastor Mt. Helm Baptist Church, a historic congregation known by academics as the fountainhead of the Black Holiness movement. Charles Price Jones, the inspiration behind this book, became our church's fifth pastor with an agenda to help it grow spiritually and morally in the midst of racial terrorism and changing times. A scholarly pastor, Jones defied the stereotype that one could not have both "learning" and "burning" within Baptist contexts. He had both and wanted all believers, regardless of denominational affiliation, to have the same. Years of denominational tensions, however, have obscured the impact Jones had on his generation of Baptists, though he was not alone in his advocacy for a Spirit-empowered ministry. Other Black Baptists in his era saw the error of the progressive social gospelers who put more trust in respectability politics than spiritual power. Though progressives like E. C. Morris and Jones agreed that Black people needed liberal arts education, economic enterprise, and moral character, they disagreed on the motivation and source of such uplift. Morris and others sought critical assimilation into dominant society; Jones risked being misunderstood within both White and Black cultures for wanting something deeper: the fullness of the Holy Spirit.

To be sure, as Baptists we believe that those saved by Jesus have all the Spirit they will ever have. When we are baptized into Christ by the Spirit, we do not need "more of God" so much as God wants more of us. But this does not contradict Paul's admonition to be filled (continually) with the Holy Spirit (Ephesians 5:18). If we want greater peace, greater power, greater productivity, we should humble ourselves and pray daily to be filled and fully influenced by the Holy Spirit of God. Ultimately, I believe this was Jones' desire: less of me, more of You, Lord! Until pastors and the people of God enter a state of surrender, much will not change in the conditions of our churches. And if churches are to be leading institutions in our communities, we can conclude that many of the negative statistics in our homes, schools, and streets will not change much. A revived church is God's means for an awakened society.

Though I grew up an and was shaped by a Christian home, profound doubts about the veracity of Scripture and concerns about so many evils in the world led me on a spiritual quest to find a "better way" beyond my native religion during my teenage years. I studied Eastern religions and Western philosophies and found greater meaning in them than I did the Bible. I suppose I could have been called "spiritual but not religious," except for the fact that I had serious reservations about believing that God, by whatever name, existed. That wandering ended when the Lord Jesus Christ powerfully overwhelmed every reason *not* to believe in him through signs and wonders. Since that time, God has used me to offer words of knowledge and wisdom, to have dreams and visions, and other things that may be mocked in some Baptist settings. I have been ridiculed by Pentecostals for remaining in my "tribe." But by God's grace I am called to be a reformer. I love the Black Baptist tradition. It has meant so much to my upbringing and to the welfare of my people. One of my heroes, Rev. Dr. Martin Luther King Jr., was a Baptist minister. I love our hymns, our rituals, our whooping. What I've encountered, though, I want all of us to encounter. I believe revival is coming to the Baptist church and it will be marvelous in our eyes. Imagine declining churches once again filled with people, baptismal pools filled every week, godly sorrow over sin, restored relationships, deliverance from addictions and healing from diseases. Imagine "justice rolling down like waters and righteousness like a mighty steam." (Amos 5:24) Imagine spiritual and truthful worship that is free, liberating, and life-altering. Imagine churches alive with the glory of the Lord.

By God's grace, we can get to that place through humility. Surrendered lives are always candidates for divine power. In order to get there, we will need to trust there is no inherent contradiction between the Word and the Spirit. Adrian Roger, in *The Incredible Power of Kingdom Authority*, preaches

> There are some people, however, who have made an artificial distinction between the authority of the holy Scriptures and the authority of the Holy Spirit. This is so foolish because it is the Holy Spirit who inspired the Scriptures and he is the one who opens them to our heart. Therefore, it is not the Spirit or the Word but the Spirit *and* the Word. We're to worship our Lord in Spirit and in truth.

Bapticostal—this compound of Baptist and Pentecostal that speaks to the reuniting of Word and Spirit—betrays the truth of the historic record, which is that from Baptist origins to this present age, many Baptists savored the dynamic empowerment of the Holy Ghost for mission, piety, and worship. The thousands of National Baptist churches that now identify as Full Gospel Baptists, and myriad congregations whose cultures are reminiscent of the

Sanctified church, have long been a part of this denomination and prefer the title Baptist to anything else. They seek deeper spiritual empowerment, more fire to burn up everything not like God in them, to have a religion they can feel sometimes. These have been anointed leaders who haven't forgot how to burn. They didn't forget their own Pentecostal experience when the Lord baptized them with Holy Ghost fire. They never forgot the one who John the Baptist said would baptize us with Spirit and with fire. They remember and pattern their lives after that first century fire starter, Jesus, the Light of the world. They didn't forget the fire baptized history of Baptists who prayed, moaned, shrieked, shouted, prophesied, danced, cried, clapped, swayed, prostrated, sang, and preached in the fires of Holy Ghost revival.

Since researching and writing the dissertation upon which this book is based, I have received countless words of encouragement from Baptist pastors and lay people regarding this subject. The term "Bapticostal" is becoming more mainstream. The longing for passionate, anointed ministry is yearned for. Even allusions from Dr. Jerry Young, our present National Baptist president, gives signs of hope that the Convention is more open to these matters than it was in 1895 or 1995.

My hope is that this book calls you to remember and to seek the fullness of the Spirit. Pray that God would grow more spiritual fruit in us and demonstrate more spiritual power through us. In these unsettling times in which so much disruption is making way for new models, the Black church in America must be agile, adaptive, and responsive. I believe we can do that, not in our strength alone, but in the power of the Holy Spirit.

Deeper, deeper! tho' it cost hard trials,
Deeper let me go!
Rooted in the holy love of Jesus,
Let me fruitful grow.

About the Author

Dr. CJ Rhodes is the Pastor of Mt. Helm Baptist Church in Jackson, MS and serves as a professor at Alcorn State University. He received a BA in Philosophy from the University of Mississippi, a MDiv from Duke University Divinity School, and a Doctor of Ministry from Wesley Biblical Seminary.

He is a lead organizer for Word and Spirit Baptists, a renewal movement of biblically sound, charismatic Baptist leaders, and a prominent Christian educator, radio personality, and civic leader.

CJ is married to Allison and they are the parents of twin sons.

Bibliography

Alexander, Estrelda Y. *Black Fire: One Hundred Years of African American Pentecostalism*. Downers Grove, IL: InterVarsity Press, 2011.

Alexander, Estrelda Y., and Amos Yong, eds., *Afro-Pentecostalism: Black Pentecostal and Charismatic Christianity in History and Culture*. New York: New York University Press, 2011.

Allison, Gregg R., *Sojourners and Strangers: The Doctrine of the Church*. Wheaton, IL: Crossway, 2012.

Anyabwile, Thabiti. *Reviving the Black Church: A Call to Reclaim a Sacred Institution*. Nashville, TN: B&H Publishing, 2015.

Baldwin, Lewis V. and Victor Andersons (eds.). *Revives My Soul Again: The Spirituality of Martin Luther King Jr.* Minneapolis, MN: Fortress Press, 2018.

Bebbington, David W. *Baptists Through the Centuries: A History of a Global People*. Waco, TX: Baylor University Press, 2010.

Blackaby, Henry T., and Richard Blackaby. *Spiritual Leadership: Moving People on God's Agenda*. Nashville, TN: B&H Publishing Group, 2011.

Boothe, Charles Octavius. *Plain Theology for Plain People.* Bellingham, WA: Lexham Press, 2017.

Brueggemann, Walter. *The Prophetic Imagination.* 2nd ed. Minneapolis: Fortress Press, 2001.

Bunch, Clarence. "Servant Leadership and African American Pastors." Ph.D. diss., Antioch University, January, 2013.

Castilla, Willenham. *Moving Forward on God's Highway: A Textbook History of the Church of Christ (Holiness) U.S.A.* Bloomington, IN: AuthorHouse, 2007.

Campolo, Tony. *How to be a Pentecostal without Speaking in Tongues.* Dallas, TX: Word Publishing, 1991.

Chan, Francis. *Forgotten God: Reserving Our Tragic Neglect of the Holy Spirit.* Colorado Springs, CO: David Cook, 2009.

Chute, Anthony and Nathan A. Finn and Michael A. G. Haykin. *The Baptist Story: From English Sect to Global Movement.* B&H Academic, 2015.

Clemmons, Ithiel C. *Bishop C. H. Mason and the Roots of the Church of God in Christ.* Lanham, MD: Pneuma Life Publishing, 1996.

Cobbins, Otho B. *History of Church of Christ (Holiness) U.S.A. 1895-1965.* Vantage Press, 1966.

Cox, Harvey Gallagher. *Fire from Heaven: The Rise of Pentecostal Spirituality and the Reshaping of Religion in the Twenty-First Century*. Reading, MA: Addison-Wesley, 1995.

Deats, Richard. *Martin Luther King, Jr.: Spirit-Led Prophet: A Biography*. New City Press, 2000.

DuBois, W. E. B. *The Souls of Black Folk*. Fawcett Premier Book, 1968.

Evans, James H. Jr. *We Have Been Believers: An African-American Systematic Theology*. Minneapolis: Fortress Press, 1992.

Fee, Gordon D. *Paul, the Spirit, and the People of God*. Grand Rapids, MI: Baker Academic, 1996.

Ferguson, Sinclair B. *The Holy Spirit: Contours of Christian Theology*. Downers, IL: InterVarsity Press, 1996.

Fitts, LeRoy. *A History of Black Baptists*. Broadman Press, 1985.

Floyd-Thomas, Stacey, and Juan Floyd-Thomas. *Black Church Studies: An Introduction*. Nashville: Abingdon Press, 2007.

Fluker, Walter Earl. *Ethical Leadership: The Quest for Character, Civility, and Community*. Minneapolis, MN: Fortress Press, 2009.

Forbes, James. *The Holy Spirit and Preaching*. Nashville, TN: Abingdon Press, 1989.

Foster, Richard. *Celebration of Disciplines*. New York, NY: HarperCollins Publishers, 1998.

Franklin, Robert M. *Another Day's Journey: Black Churches Confronting the American Crisis*. Minneapolis: Augsburg Fortress Publishers, 1997.

_____. *Crisis in the Village: Restoring Hope in African American Communities*. Minneapolis: Fortress Press, 2007.

Frazier, E. Franklin, and C. Eric Lincoln. *The Negro Church in America/The Black Church Since Frazier*. New York: Schocken Books, 1974.

Full Gospel Baptist Church Fellowship International. "What We Believe – Full Gospel Distinctives." Accessed October 31, 2017. http://fullgospelbaptist.org/what-we-believe/.

Garrett, Jr., James Leo. *We Baptists: One Lord, One Faith, One Baptism*. Study and Research Division, Baptist World Alliance, 1999.

Gaillardetz, Richard. *Ecclesiology for a Global Church: A People Called and Sent*. Orbis, 2008.

Giggie, John M. *After Redemption: Jim Crow and the Transformation of African American Religion in the Delta 1875-1915*. Oxford University Press, 2008.

Goodwin, Everett C. *The New Hiscox Guide for Baptist Churches.* Valley Forge: Judson Press, 1995.

Gordon, A. J. *The Ministry of the Spirit.* Philadelphia, PA: American Baptist Society, 1894.

Graham, Billy. *The Holy Spirit: Activating God's Power in Your Life.* Nashville, TN: Thomas Nelson, 1988.

Greenleaf, Robert K. *Servant Leadership: A Journey into the Nature of Legitimate Power and Greatness.* New York, NY: Paulist Press, 1977.

Greenman, Jeffrey P., and George Kalantzis, eds. *Life in the Spirit: Spiritual Formation in Theological Perspective.* Downers Grove, IL: InterVarsity Press, 2010.

Greear, J. D. *Jesus, Continued...: Why the Spirit Inside You is Better than Jesus Inside You.* Grand Rapids, MI: Zondervan, 2014.

Guder, Darrell L. (editor). *Missional Church: A Vision for the Sending of the Church in North America.* Grand Rapids: Wm. B. Eerdmans Publishing Co., 1998.

Guns, Geoffrey V. *Spiritual Leadership: A Guide to Developing Spiritual Leaders in the Church.* Orman Press, 2000

Grudem, Wayne. *Systematic Theology: An Introduction to Biblical Doctrine.* Grand Rapids: Zondervan, 1994.

Hamilton, Charles V. *The Black Preacher in America.* New York, NY: Williams Morrow & Co., Inc., 1972.

Hammett, John S. *Biblical Foundations for Baptist Churches: A Contemporary Ecclesiology.* Grand Rapids: Kregel Publications, 2005.

Hart, Harold. "A Study of the Full Gospel Baptist Church Fellowship Conference." D.Min. diss., Howard University, 1996.

Harvey, Paul. *Redeeming the South: Religious Cultures and Racial Identities Among Southern Baptists 1865-1925.* Chapel Hill and London: The University of North Carolina Press, 1997.

Hauerwas, Stanley, and William H. Willimon. *The Holy Spirit.* Nashville, TN: Abingdon Press, 2015.

Headrick, Steven M. "A Case Study Examining Growth in Understanding Biblical Anointing At Faith Baptist Church." D.Min. diss., Liberty University Divinity School, 2016.

Hays, Brook and John E. Steely. *The Baptist Way of Life.* Englewood Cliffs, NJ: Prentice-Hall, 1963.

Hicks, Jr., H. Beecher. "Challenge to the African American Church: Problems and Perspectives for the Third Millennium." *The Journal of Religious Thought 51,* no. 1 (Summer-Fall 1994): 81-97.

Higginbotham, Evelyn Brooks. *Righteous Discontent: The Women's Movement in the Black Baptist Church, 1880-1920*. Harvard University Press, 1994.

Hiscox, E. T. *The New Directory for Baptist Churches* (31st ed.). Chicago, IL: Judson Press, 1962.

Jefferson, Anita Bingham. *Charles Price Jones: First Black Holiness Reformer (With a One Hundred Year Chronology of His Life)*. Self-published, 2011.

Jenkins, Philip. *The Next Christendom: The Coming of Global Christianity*. New York: Oxford University Press, 2002.

Jethani, Skye. "Apostles Today? Rediscovering the gift that leaves churches and well-connected pastors in its wake." Leadership Journal, Spring 2008. http://www.christianitytoday.com/le/2008/spring/15.37.html?paging=off

_____. *Immeasurable: Reflections on the Soul of Ministry in the Age of Church, Inc.* Chicago, IL: Moody Press, 2017.

Karkkainen, Veli-Metti, *Pneumatology: The Holy Spirit in Ecumenical, International, and Contextual Perspective*. Grand Rapids, MI: Baker Academic, 2002.

Kidd, Thomas S., and Barry Hankins. *Baptists in America: A History*. Oxford University Press, 2015.

King, Jr., Martin Luther. "I've Been to the Mountaintop." San Francisco, CA: Harper San Francisco, 1994.

_____. *Stride Toward Freedom*. Boston, MA: Beacon Press, 2010.

Lincoln, C. Eric, and Lawrence H. Mamiya. *The Black Church in the African American Experience*. Durham and London: Duke University Press, 1990.

Lumpkin, William L. *Baptist Confessions of Faith*. Valley Forge: Judson Press, 1959.

Maring, Norman H., and Winthrop S. Hudson, eds. *A Baptist Manual of Polity and Practice*. Valley Forge, PA: Judson Press, 2012.

Marshall, Molly T. *Joining the Dance: A Theology of the Spirit*. Valley Forge: Judson Press, 2003.

Massey, Floyd Jr., and Samuel Berry McKinney. *Church Administration in the Black Perspective* (rev. ed.). Valley Forge: Judson Press, 2003.

Maxwell, John. *The 21 Irrefutable Laws of Leadership: Follow Them and People Will Follow You*. Nashville, TN: Thomas Nelson, 1998.

McClendon, James Wm. Jr. *Ethics: Systematic Theology, Volume 1*. Nashville: Abingdon Press, 2002.

_____. *Doctrine: Systematic Theology, Volume 2*. Nashville: Abingdon Press, 1994.

McFarland, Allen R. "Theory and Practices in Pastoring Americans of African Descent: A Contemporary Agenda." D.Min. diss., Liberty University Divinity School, 1999.

McMickle, Marvin A. *Where Have All the Prophets Gone?: Reclaiming Prophetic Preaching in America*. Cleveland: Pilgrim Press, 2007.

McMillen, Neil R. *Dark Journey: Black Mississippians in the Age of Jim Crow*. Urbana and Chicago, IL: University of Illinois Press, 1990.

Mills, Zach. *The Last Blues Preacher: Reverend Clay Evans, Black Lives, and the Faith that Woke the Nation*. Minneapolis, MN: Fortress Press, 2018.

Moltmann, Jurgen. *The Church in the Power of the Spirit: A Contribution to Messianic Ecclesiology*. New York: Harper & Row, 1993.

_____. *The Spirit of Life: A Universal Affirmation*. Sr Albans Place, London: SCM Press, 1992.

Morris, Aldon D., and Lee, Shayne. "The National Baptist Convention: Traditions and the Challenge of Modernity." In D. A. Roozen, & J. R. Nieman (eds.), *Church, Identity, and Change: Theology and Denominational Structures in Unsettled Times* (pp. 336-379). Grand Rapids, MI: William B. Eerdmans Publishing Company, 2005.

Morris, E. C. *Sermons, Addresses and Reminiscences.* Nashville, TN: National Baptist Publishing Board, 1901.

Morton, Paul S. *Changing Forward: Experiencing God's Unlimited Power.* Nashville, TN: Abingdon Press, 2012.

Murray, Stuart. *Post-Christendom: Church and Mission in a Strange New World.* Paternoster, 2004.

Norman, Stanton. *The Baptist Way: Distinctives of a Baptist Church.* Nashville, TN: Broadman & Holman Publishers, 2005.

Nouwen, Henri J. M. *In the Name of Jesus: Reflections on Christian Leadership.* The Crossroad Publishing Company, 1989/2002.

Oden, Thomas C. *Pastoral Theology: Essentials of Ministry.* New York: HarperCollins, 1983.

Olofinjana, Israel Oluwole. *Partnership in Mission: A Black Majority Church Perspective on Mission and Church Unity.* Great Britain: Instant Apostle, 2015.

Packer, J. I. *Keep in Step with the Spirit: Finding Fullness in our Walk with God* (rev.). Grand Rapids, MI: Baker Books, 2005.

Park, Nam Ju. "Strategies for Using Spiritual Gifts in Korean Church Growth." D.Min. diss. Liberty Baptist Theological Seminary, May, 2001.

Peterson, Eugene H. *The Contemplative Pastor: Returning to the Art of Spiritual Direction.* Grand Rapids, MI: William B. Eerdmans Publishing Company, 1989.

Pinn, Anthony B. *Terror and Triumph: The Nature of Black Religion.* Minneapolis: Fortress Press, 2003.

_____. *The Black Church in the Post-Civil Rights Era.* Maryknoll, NY: Orbis Books, 2002.

Pinnock, Clark H. *Flame of Love: A Theology of the Holy Spirit.* Downers Grove, IL: Intervarsity Press, 1996.

Piper, John. *Brothers, We Are* Not *Professionals: A Plea to Pastors for Radical Ministry.* Nashville, TN: B&H Books, 2013.

Proctor, Samuel D., and Gardner C. Taylor. *We Have This Ministry: The Heart of the Pastor's Vocation.* Valley Forge: Judson Press, 1996.

Raboteau, Albert J. *Canaan Land: A Religious History of African Americans.* Oxford and New York: Oxford University Press, 1999.

Rah, Soong-Chan. *The Next Evangelicalism: Freeing the Church from Western Cultural Captivity.* IVP, 2009.

Rainer, Thom S. *Autopsy of a Deceased Church.* Nashville, TN: B&H Publishing Group, 2008.

Reeder, Diane Prcotor (ed.). *Elijah's Mantle: Empowering the Next Generation of African American Christian Leaders.* Grand Rapids, MI: Kregel Publishing, 2013.

Rogers, Adrian. *Kingdom Authority: The Incredible Power of Getting an Upper Hand on the Underworld.* Nashville, TN: B&H Publishing Group, 2002.

Robinson, Anthony B., and Robert W. Wall. *Called to be Church: The Book of Acts for a New Day.* Grand Rapids: Wm. B. Eerdmans Publishing Company, 2006.

Sanders, Cheryl J. *Saints in Exile: The Holiness-Pentecostal Experience in African American Religion and Culture.* Oxford University Press, 1996.

Sanders, J. Oswald. *Spiritual Leadership.* Chicago: Moody Press, 1976.

Savage, Barbara Dianne. *Your Spirits Walk Beside Us: The Politics of Black Religion.* The Belknap Press of Harvard University Press, 2008.

Sernett, Milton C. (editor). *African American Religious History: Documentary Witness* (2d ed.). Durham and London: Duke University Press, 1999.

Shalian, Michael John. "Transformational Leadership in Church Revitalization: A Study of Heights Church in Beech Island, South Carolina." Ph.D. diss., Tennessee Temple University, 2013.

Sider, Ronald J., Philip N. Olson and Heidi Rolland Unruh. *Churches that Make a Difference: Reaching Your Community with Good News and Good Works.* Grand Rapids, MI: Baker Books, 2002.

Smart, Robert Davis, Michael A. G. Haykin, and Ian High Clary (eds.). *Pentecostal Outpourings: Revival and the Reformed Tradition.* Grand Rapids, MI: Reformation Heritage Books, 2   2016.

Smith, Raynard D. Smith (ed.). *With Signs Following: The Life and Ministry of Charles Harrison Mason.* St. Louis, MI: Christian Board of Publication, 2015.

Sparks, Randy J. *Religion in Mississippi.* Jackson, MS: University Press of Mississippi, 2001.

Spener, Philip Jacob. *Pia Desideria* (trans., ed. by Theodore G. Tappert). Fortress Press, 1964.

Spurgeon, Charles H. *Lectures to My Students.* Zondervan, 1979.

Storms, Sam. *Practicing the Power: Welcoming the Gifts of the Holy Spirit in Your Life.* Grand Rapids, MI: Zondervan, 2017.

Synan, Vinson. *The Century of the Holy Spirit: 100 Years of Pentecostal and Charismatic Renewal.* Nashville, TN: Thomas Nelson, 2001.

Taylor, Charles. *A Secular Age*. The Belknap Press of Harvard University Press, 2007.

Thompson, Patrick H. *The History of Negro Baptists in Mississippi*. Jackson, MS, 1898.

Thurman, Howard (ed. Luther E. Smith Jr). *Essential Writings*. Maryknoll, NY: Orbis Books, 2006.

Tolbert, Malcolm O. *Shaping the Church: Adapting New Testament Models for Today*. Macon, GA: Smyth & Helwys Publishing, Inc., 2003.

The Mississippi Constitution of 1890. The Mississippi Historical Society.

Tribble, Sherman Roosevelt (ed.). *Total Praise: Songs and Other Worship Resources for Every Generation*. Chicago, IL: GIA Publications, 2011.

Turner, Jr. William C. *A Journey through the Church Covenant: Discipleship for African American Christians*. Valley Forge, PA: Judson Press, 2002.

_____. *The United Holy Church of America*. Piscataway, NJ: Gorgias Press, 2006.

Van Gelder, Craig. *The Essence of the Church: A Community Created by the Spirit*. Baker Books, 2000.

Vickers, Jason E. *Minding the Good Ground: A Theology for Church Renewal*. Waco, TX: Baylor University Press, 2011.

Walker, Joseph W. III. *Leadershifts: Mastering Transitions in Leadership & Life*. Nashville: Abingdon Press, 2014.

Warnock, Raphael G. *The Divided Mind of the Black Church: Theology, Piety & Witness*. New York: New York University Press, 2014.

Washington, James Melvin. *Frustrated Fellowship: The Black Baptist Quest for Social Power*. Mercer University Press, 1991.

Weaver, C. Douglas. *Baptists and the Holy Spirit: The Contested History with Holiness-Pentecostal-Charismatic Movements*. Waco, TX: Baylor Press, 2019.

Weems, Lovett H. *Leadership in the Wesleyan Spirit*. Nashville: Abingdon Press, 1999.

Williams, J. Rodman. *Renewal Theology: Systematic Theology from a Charismatic Perspective*. Zondervan, 1996.

Williams, John H. *Black Baptists in Mississippi: A Historical Perspective, Vol. 1*. Self-published, 1992.

_____. *Black Baptists in Mississippi: The Tragedy of Unkept Vineyards, Vol. II*. Self-published, 1993.

Williams, Juan, and Quinton Dixie. *The Far by Faith: Stories from the African American Religious Experience*. New York, NY: Amistad Press, 2003.

Williams, Lee. *Mt. Helm Baptist Church 1835-1988: The Parade of Pastors 1864-1988*. Jackson, MS: Mount Helm Baptist Church, 1988.

Willimon, William H. *Pastor: The Theology and Practice of Ordained Ministry*. Nashville: Abingdon Press, 2002.

Wills, Gregory A. "The Ecclesiology of Charles H. Spurgeon: Unity, Orthodoxy, and Denominational Identity." In Midwestern Journal of Theology, Fall 2015, vol. 14, no. 2.

White, Calvin Jr. *The Rise to Respectability: Race, Religion, and the Church of God in Christ*. The University of Arkansas Press, 2012.

Woodson, Carter Godwin. *The History of the Negro Church*. Washington, D.C.: Associated Publishers, 1921.

Yong, Amos. *Renewing Christian Theology: Systematics for a Global Christianity*. Waco, TX: Baylor University Press, 2014.

_____. *The Spirit Poured Out on All Flesh: Pentecostalism and the Possibility of Global Theology*. Grand Rapids, MI: Baker Academic, 2005.

Young, Jerry. "A study of pastoral leadership development training within the Jackson District Missionary Baptist Association." D.Min. diss., Reformed Theological Seminary, 1998.

Made in the USA
Middletown, DE
06 October 2020